FOR ORGANS, PIANOS & ELECTRONIC KEYBOARDS

80

THE ESSENTIAL
Paul Anka

T0052955

CONTENTS

Cover photo from the Frank Driggs Collection

ISBN 0-634-07962-X

7777 W. Bluemound Rd. P.O. Box 13819 Milwaukee, WI 53213

Visit Hal Leonard Online at
www.halleonard.com

Diana

Registration 7
Rhythm: Rock or 8 Beat

Words and Music by
Paul Anka

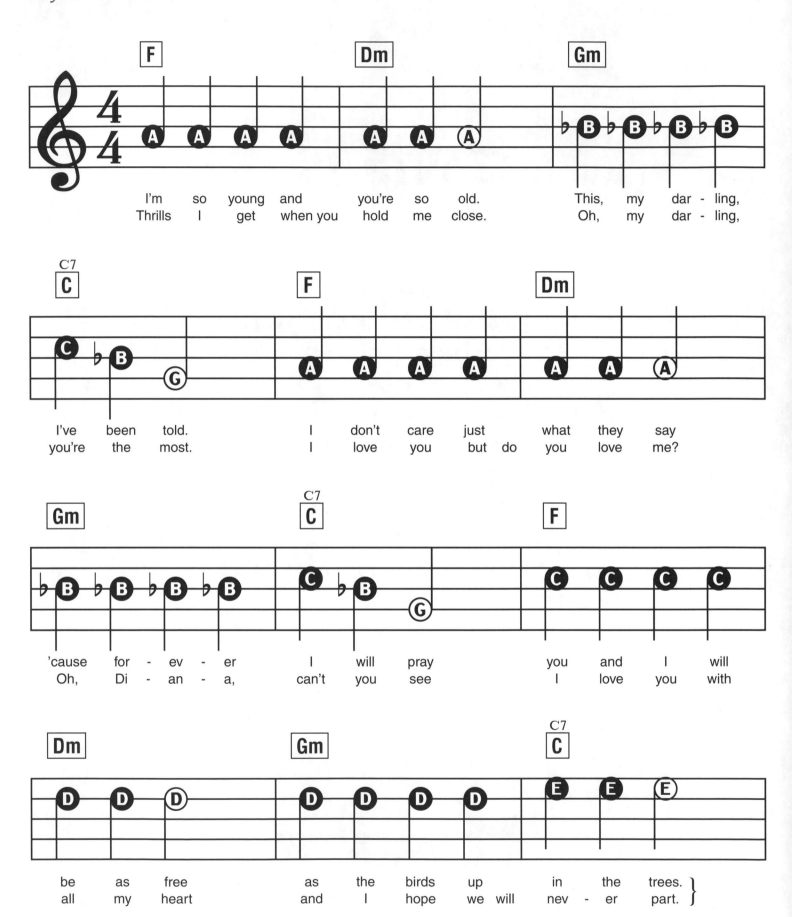

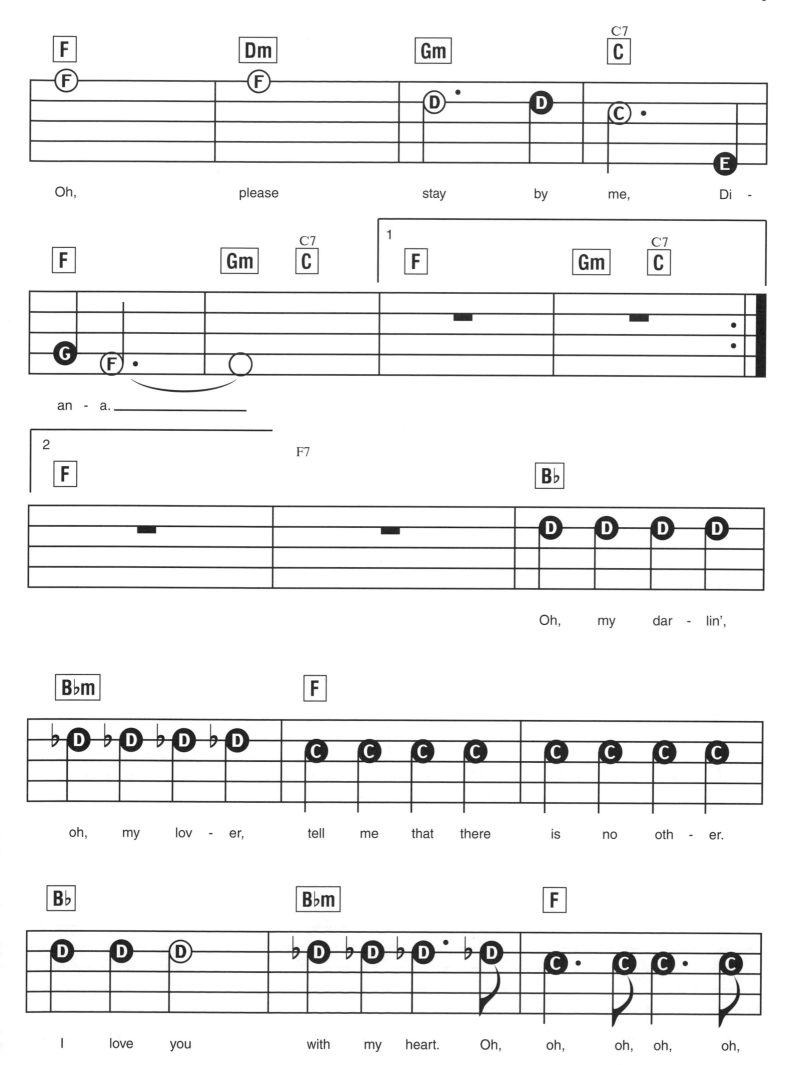

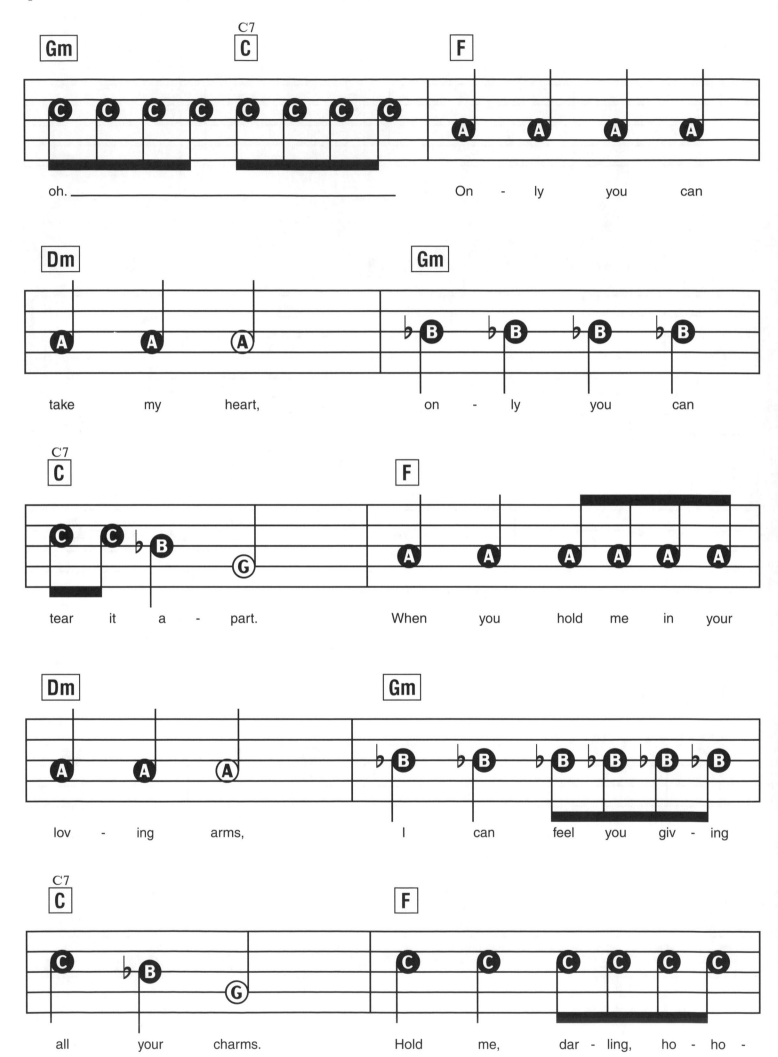

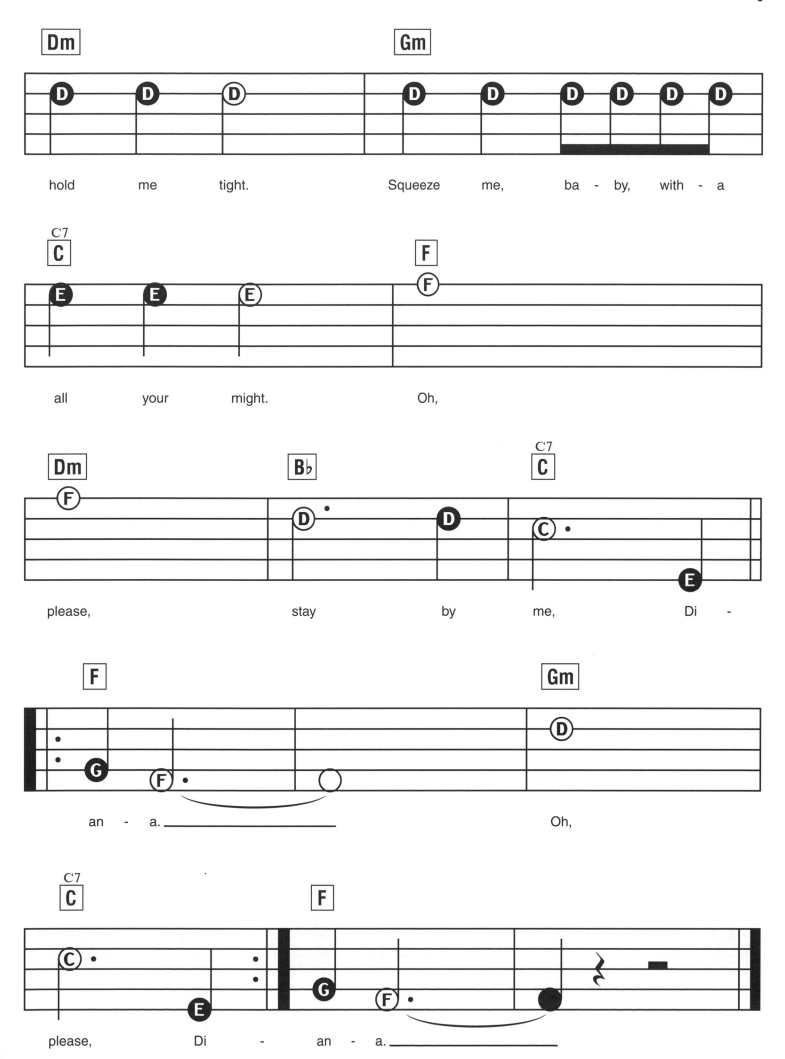

(You're)
Having My Baby

Registration 1
Rhythm: Ballad or 8 Beat

Words and Music by
Paul Anka

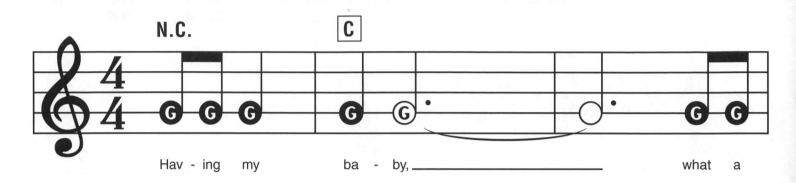

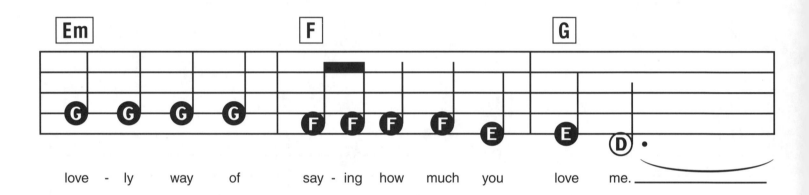

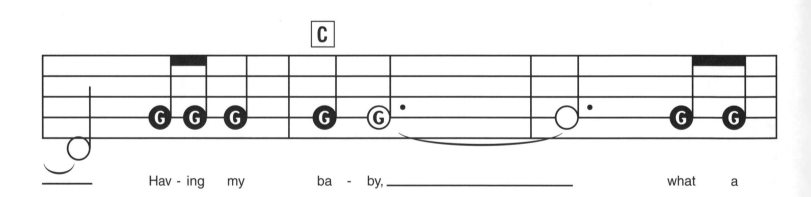

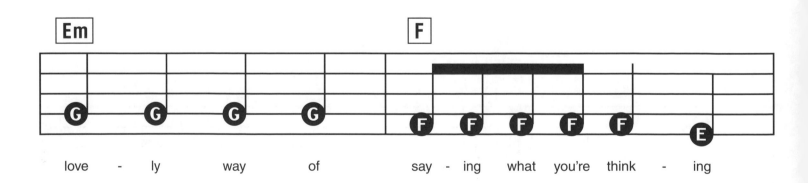

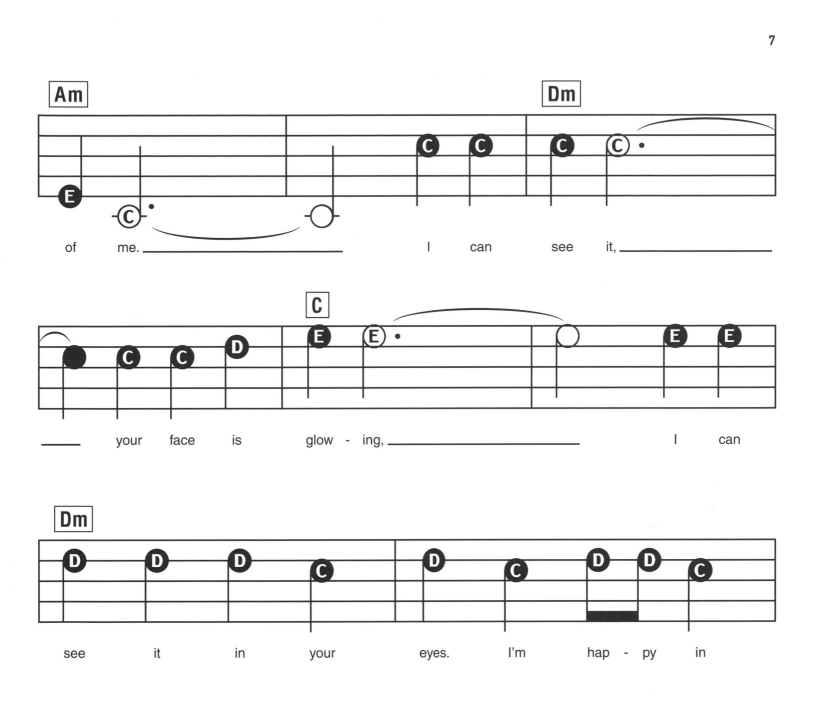

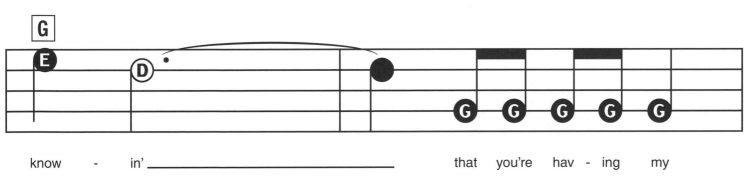

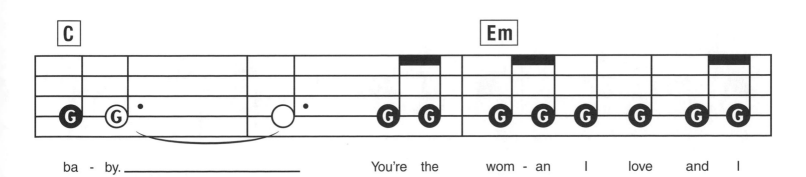

8

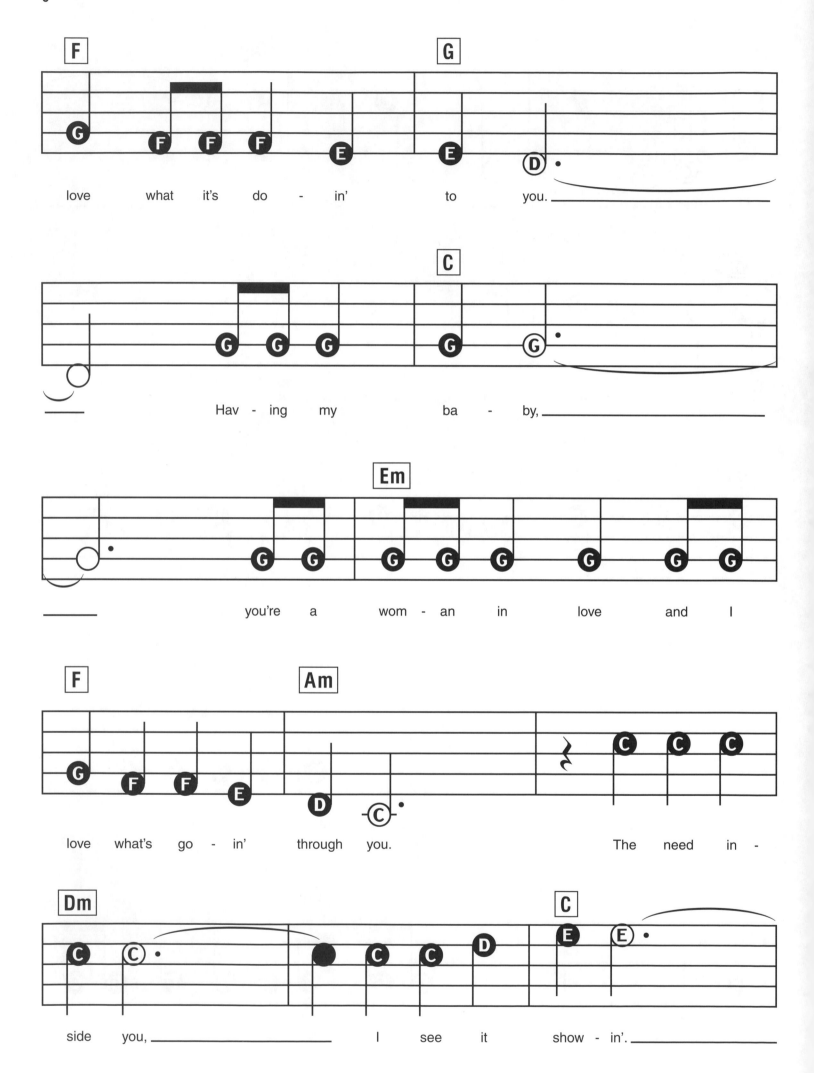

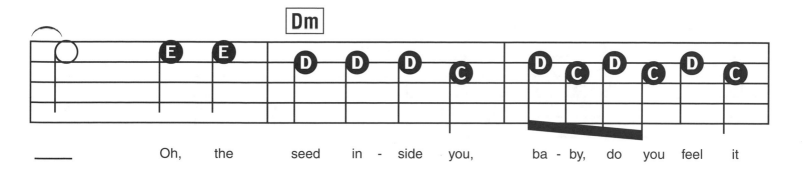

Oh, the seed in - side you, ba - by, do you feel it

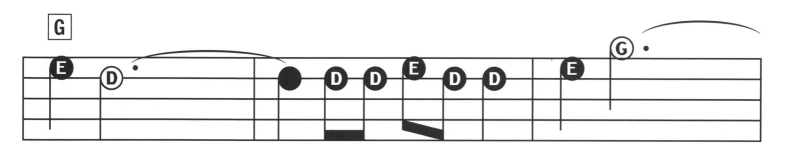

grow - in'? _____ Are you hap - py in know - in' _____

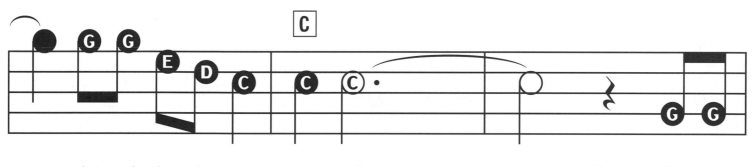

_____ that you're hav - ing my ba - by? _____ *Female:* (I'm a

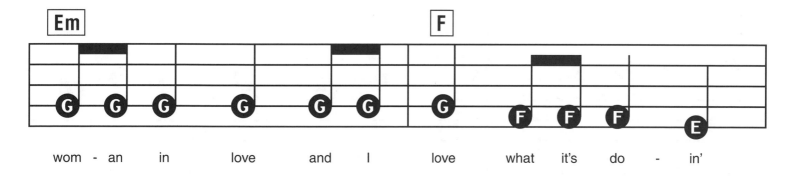

wom - an in love and I love what it's do - in'

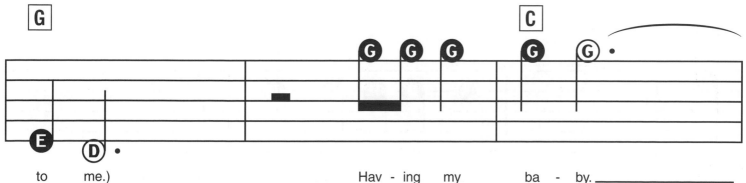

to me.) Hav - ing my ba - by. _____

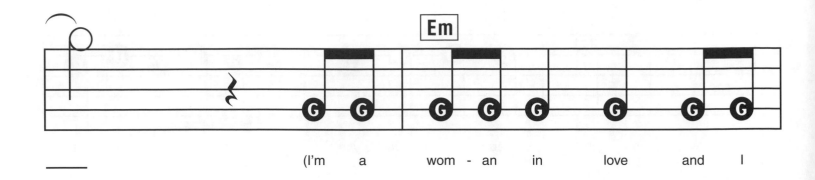

(I'm   a   wom - an   in   love   and   I

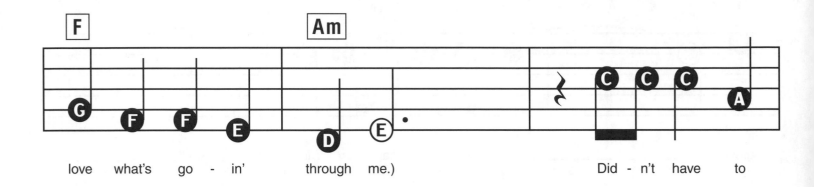

love   what's   go - in'   through   me.)   Did - n't   have   to

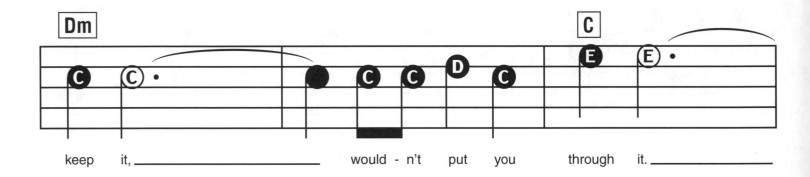

keep   it, _____   would - n't   put   you   through   it. _____

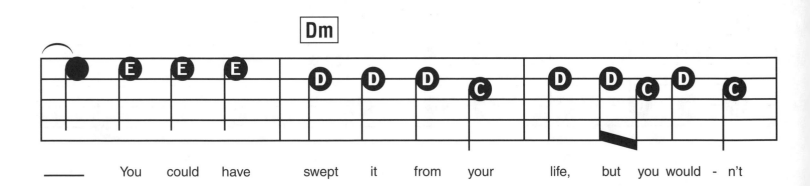

__   You   could   have   swept   it   from   your   life,   but   you   would - n't

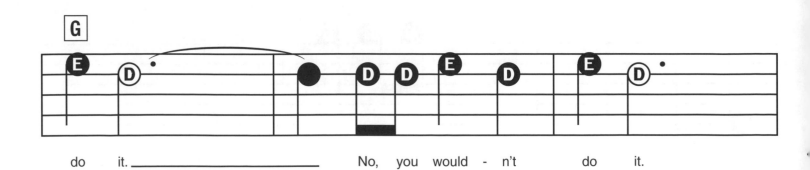

do   it. _____   No,   you   would - n't   do   it.

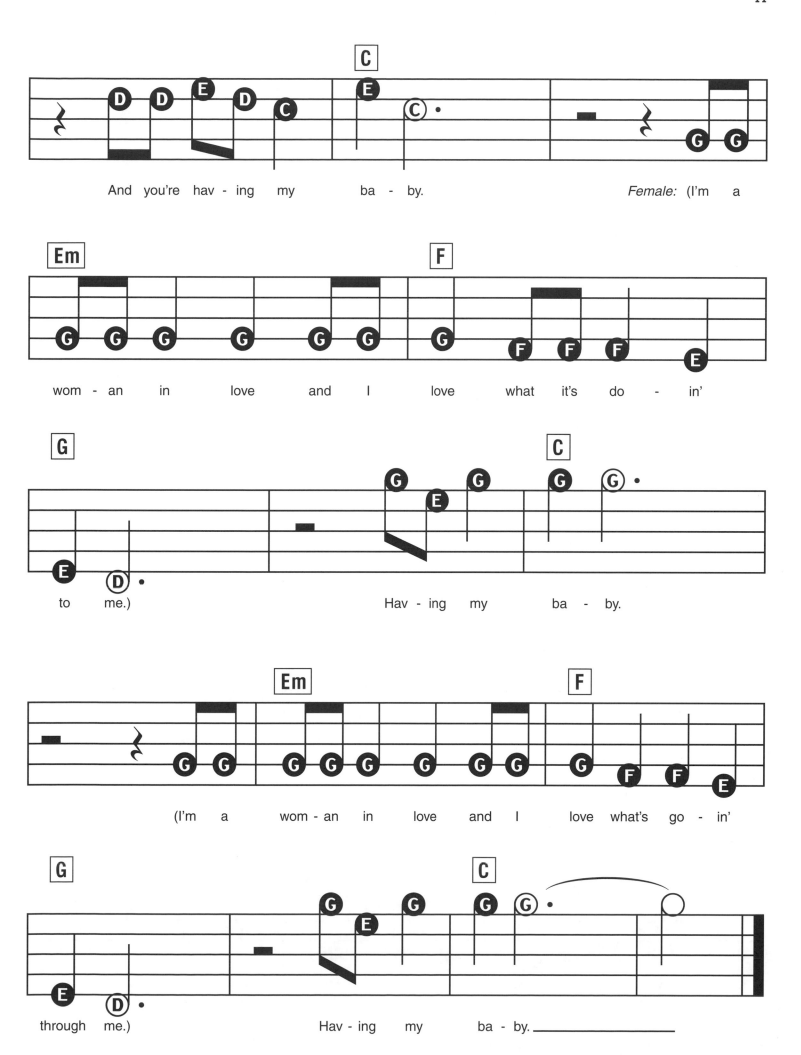

And you're hav-ing my ba - by.   Female: (I'm a

wom - an in love and I love what it's do - in'

to me.)   Hav - ing my ba - by.

(I'm a wom - an in love and I love what's go - in'

through me.)   Hav - ing my ba - by. _____

Hold Me 'Til the Mornin' Comes

Registration 8
Rhythm: 4/4 Ballad or Rock

Words and Music by David Foster
and Paul Anka

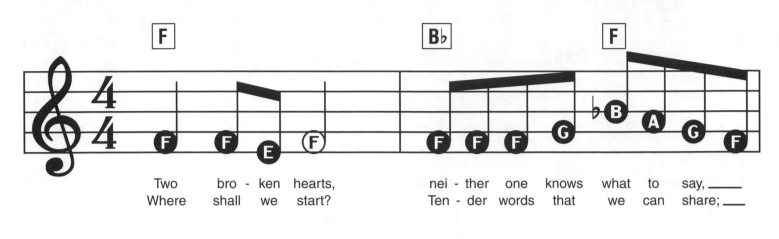

Two bro - ken hearts, nei - ther one knows what to say, ____
Where shall we start? Ten - der words that we can share; ____

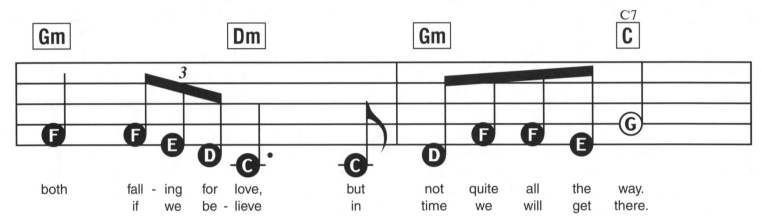

both fall - ing for love, but not quite all the way.
if we be - lieve in time we will get there.

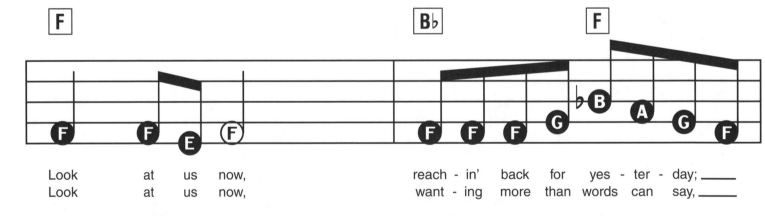

Look at us now, reach - in' back for yes - ter - day; ____
Look at us now, want - ing more than words can say, ____

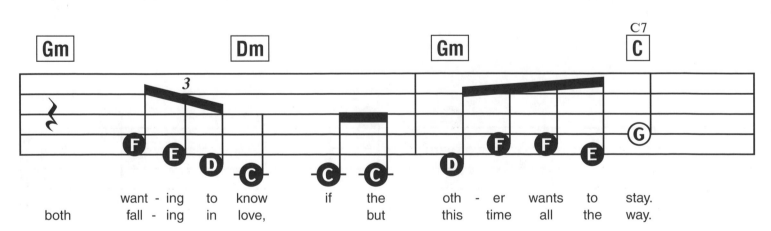

want - ing to know if the oth - er wants to stay.
both fall - ing in love, but this time all the way.

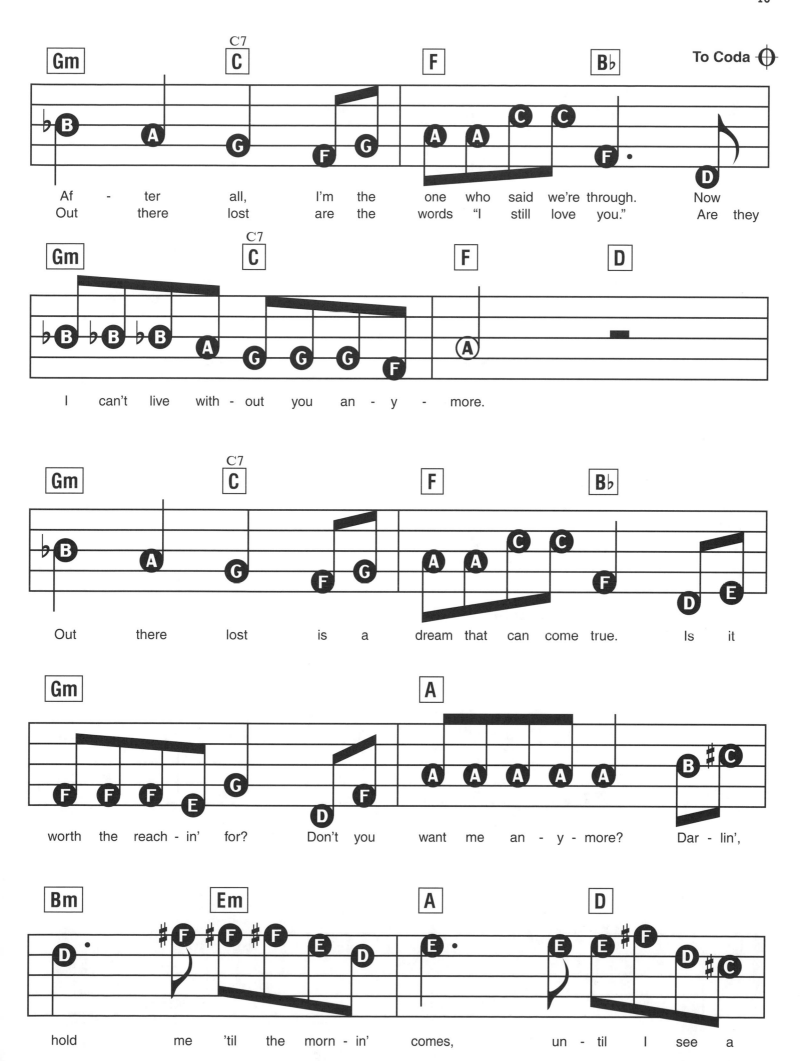

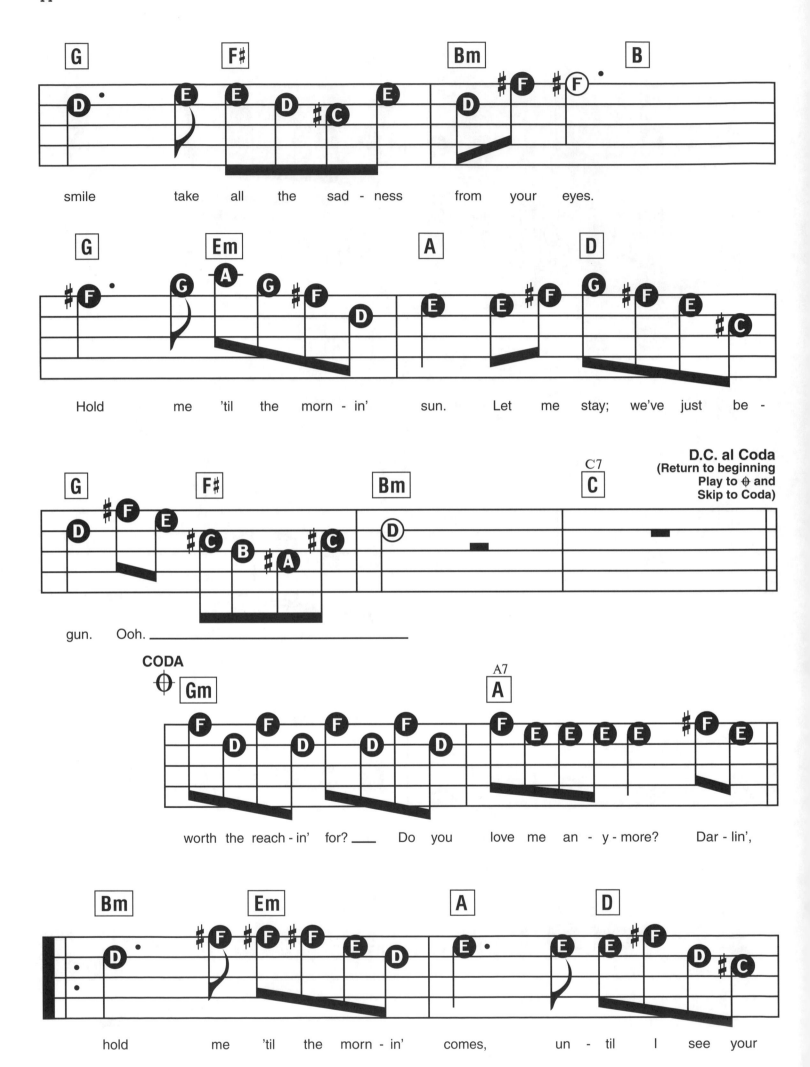

15

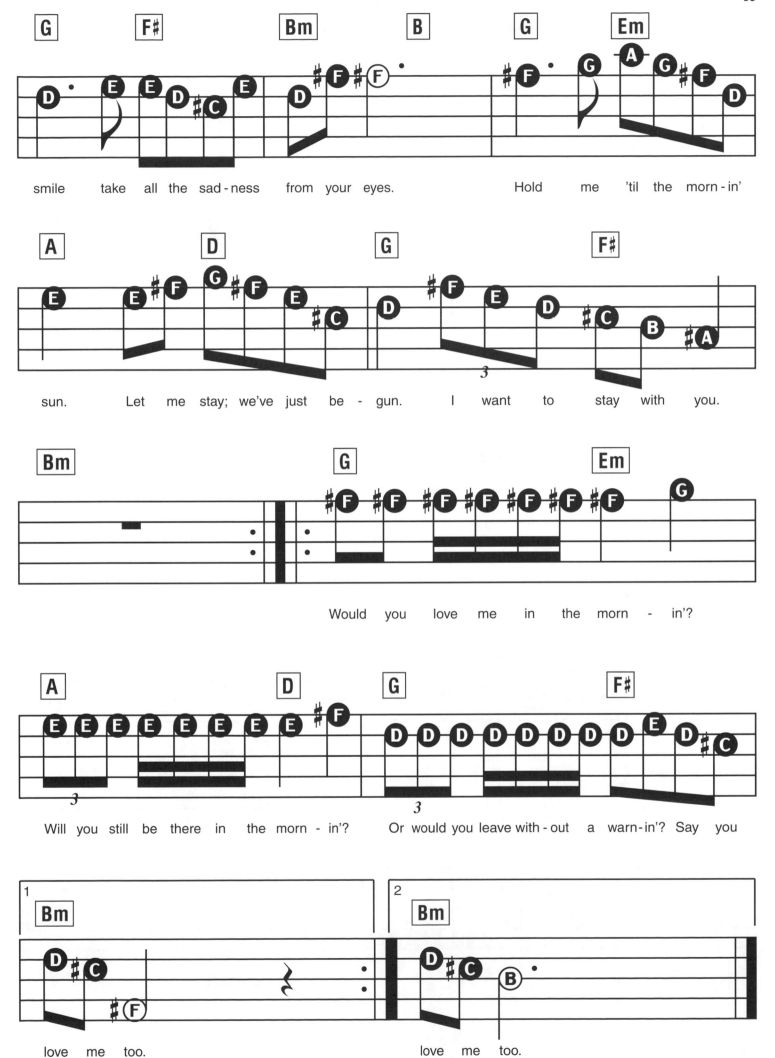

It Doesn't Matter Any More

Registration 8
Rhythm: 8 Beat or Rock

Words and Music by
Paul Anka

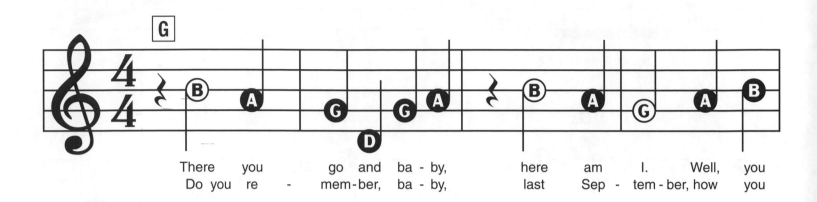

There you go and ba - by, here am I. Well, you
Do you re - mem - ber, ba - by, last Sep - tem - ber, how you

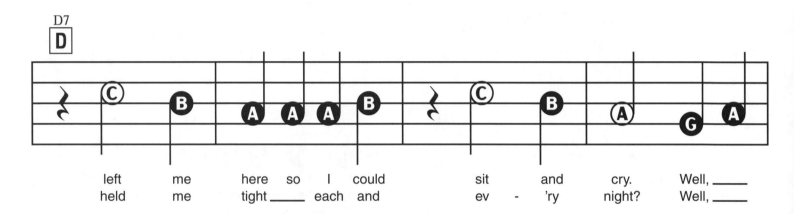

left me here so I could sit and cry. Well, _____
held me tight _____ each and ev - 'ry night? Well, _____

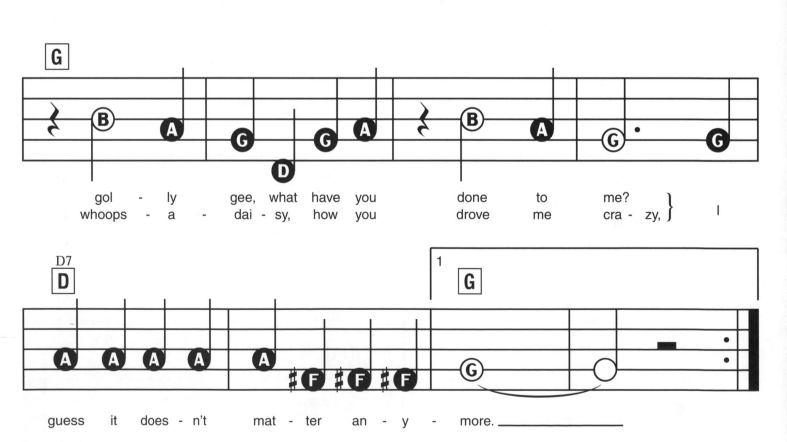

gol - ly gee, what have you done to me?
whoops - a - dai - sy, how you drove me cra - zy, }

1.

guess it does - n't mat - ter an - y - more. _____

17

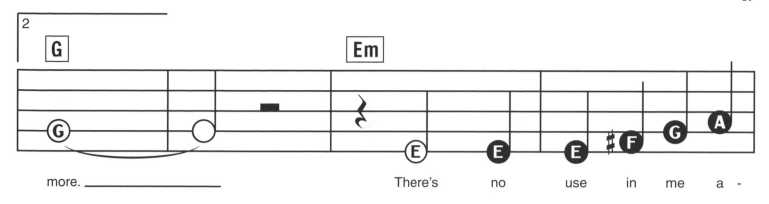

more. _____ There's no use in me a -

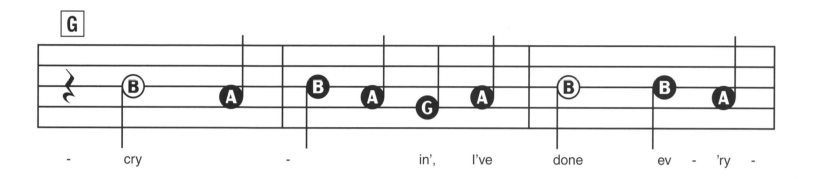

\- cry - in', I've done ev - 'ry -

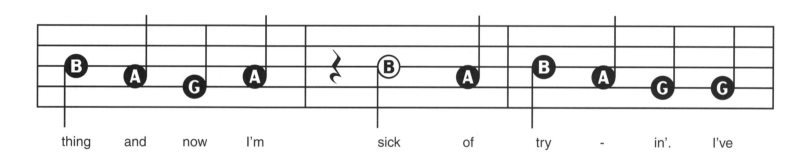

thing and now I'm sick of try - in'. I've

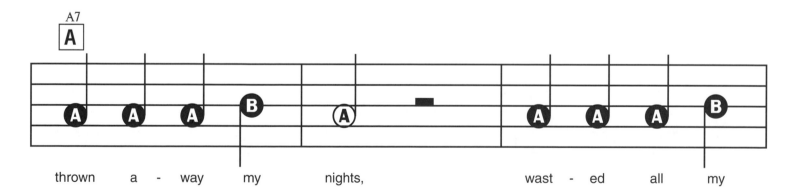

thrown a - way my nights, wast - ed all my

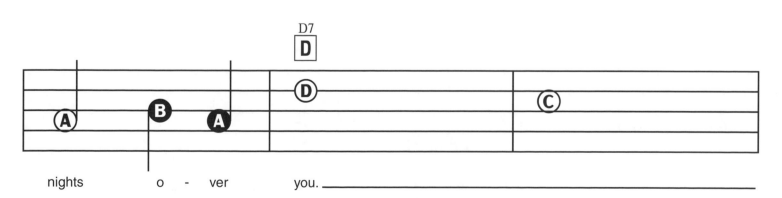

nights o - ver you. _____

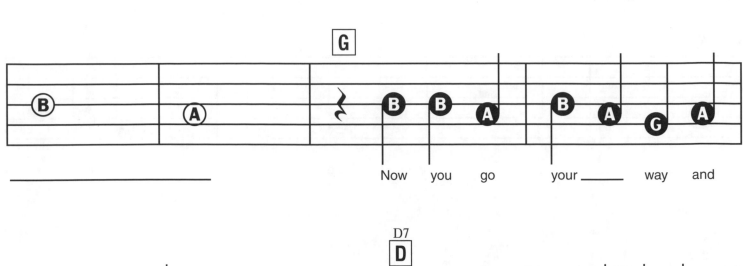

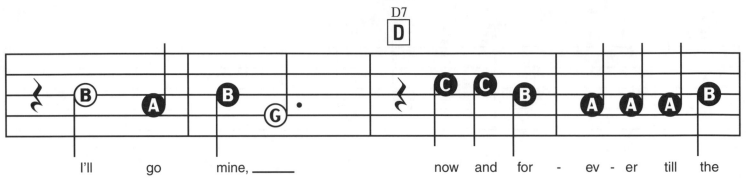

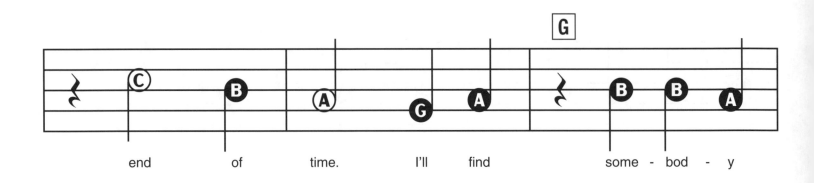

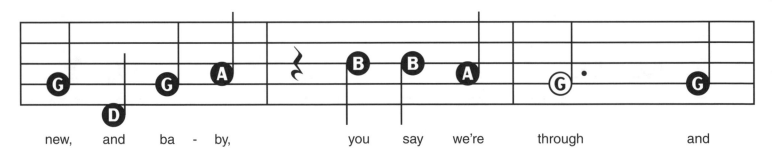

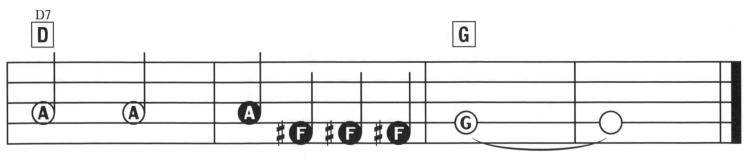

Let Me Try Again

Registration 1
Rhythm: Rock or Ballad

English Lyrics by Paul Anka and Sammy Cahn
Music by Caravelli, Michel Jourdan and Romvald Figuier

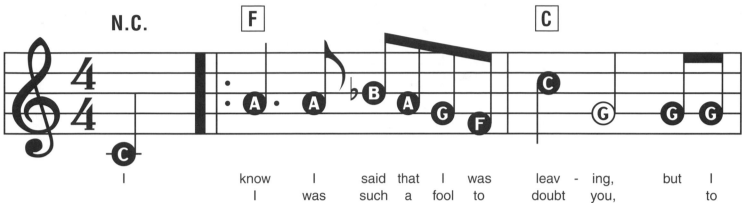

I know I said that I was leav - ing, but I
I was such a fool to doubt you, to

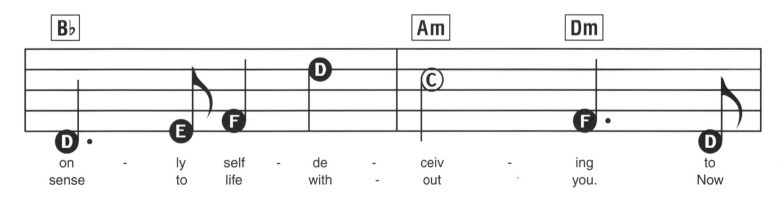

just could - n't say good - bye. It was
try to go it all a - lone. There's no

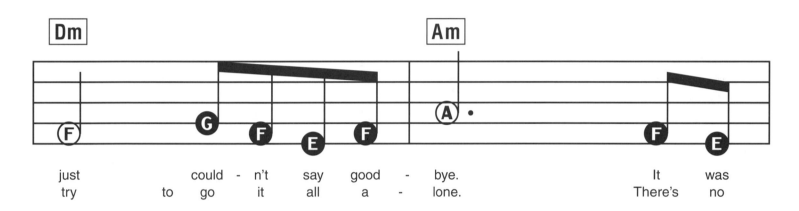

on - ly self - de - ceiv - ing to
sense to life with - out you. Now

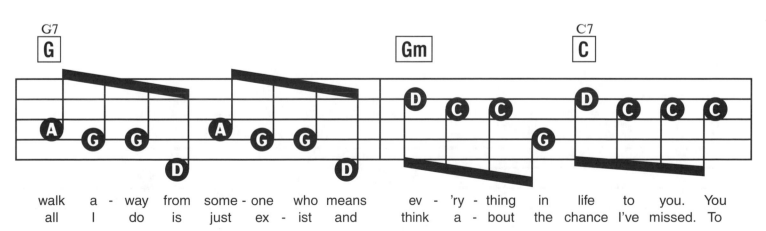

walk a - way from some - one who means ev - 'ry - thing in life to you. You
all I do is just ex - ist and think a - bout the chance I've missed. To

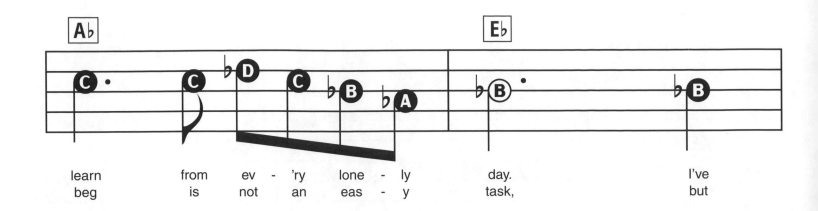

learn from ev - 'ry lone - ly day. I've
beg is not an eas - y task, but

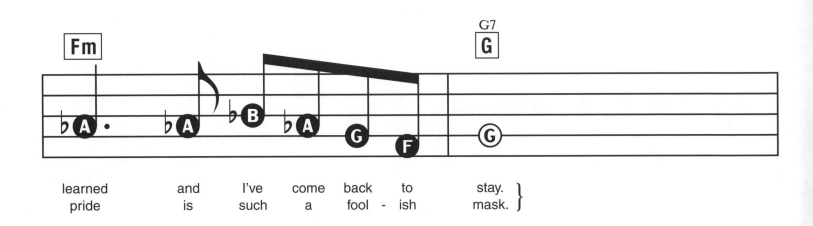

learned and I've come back to stay.
pride is such a fool - ish mask.

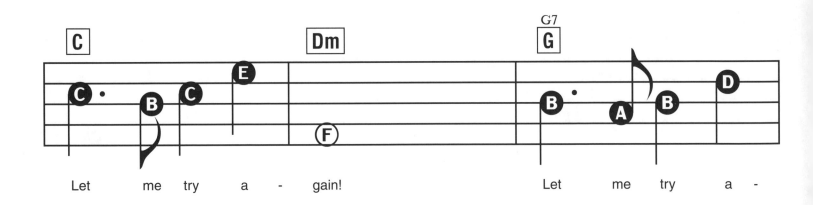

Let me try a - gain! Let me try a -

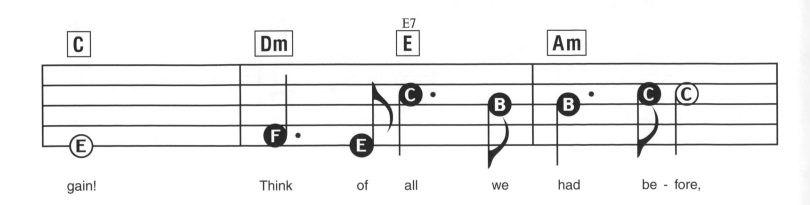

gain! Think of all we had be - fore,

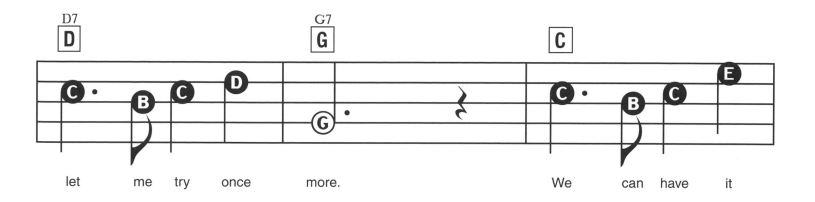

let me try once more.　　　　We can have it

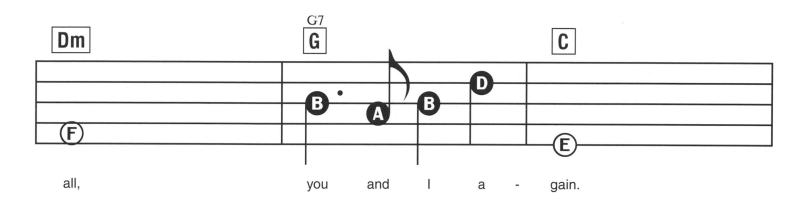

all,　　　　you and I a - gain.

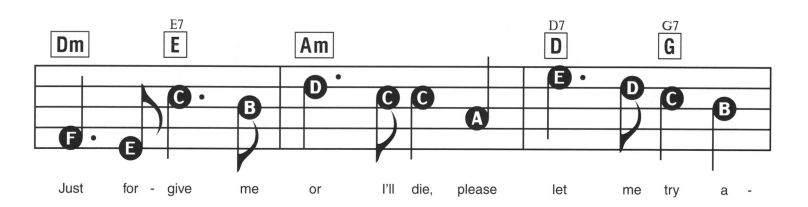

Just for - give me or I'll die, please let me try a -

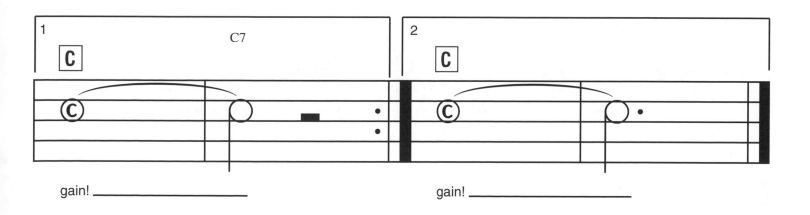

gain! _____　　　gain! _____

Johnny's Theme

Registration 2
Rhythm: Swing

Words and Music by Paul Anka
and Johnny Carson

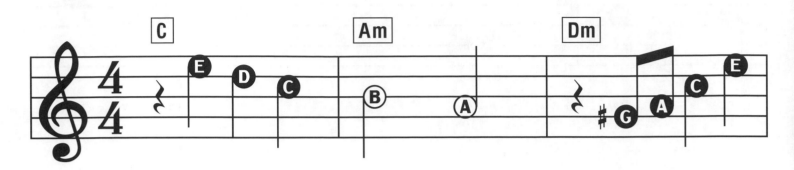

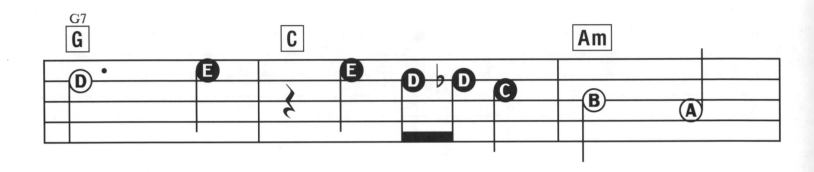

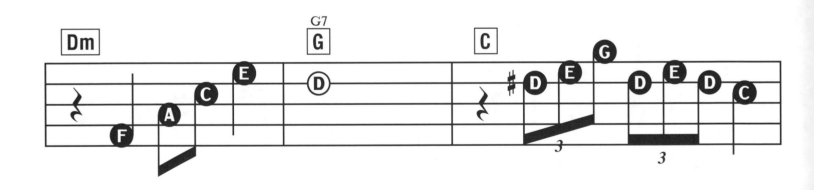

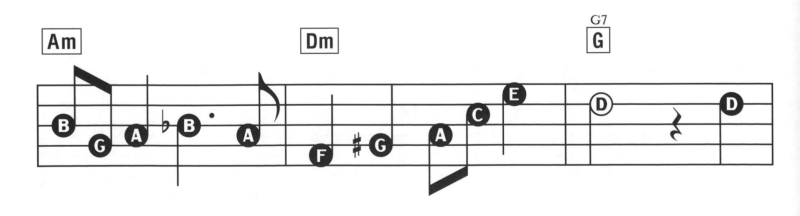

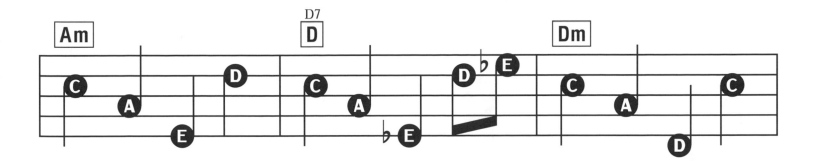

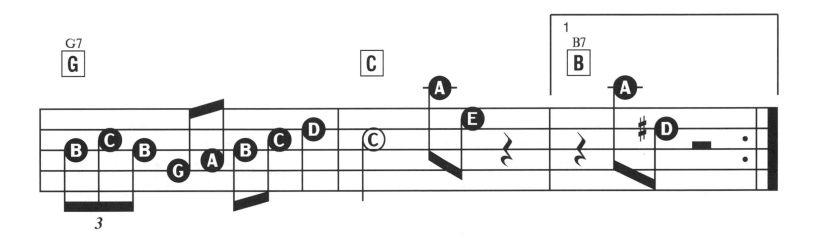

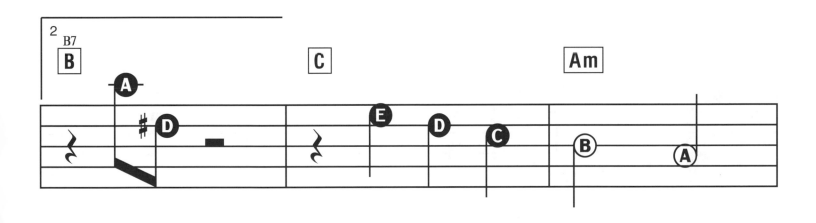

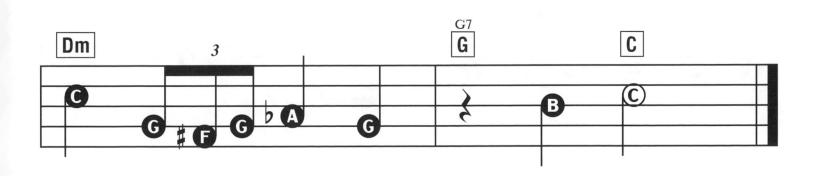

Jubilation

Registration 8
Rhythm: 8 Beat or Rock

Words and Music by Paul Anka
and Johnny Harris

Great ju - bi - la - tion, there's   some cel - e - bra - tion be -
Peo - ple, take heart, it's the   time to be smart, to be

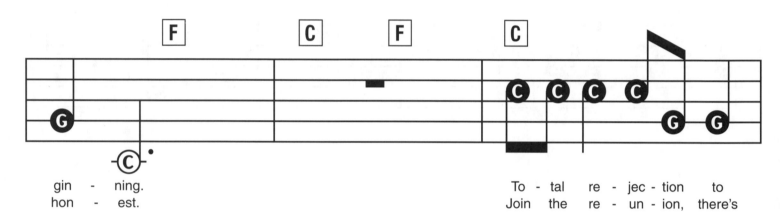

gin - ning.   To - tal re - jec - tion to
hon - est.   Join the re - un - ion, there's

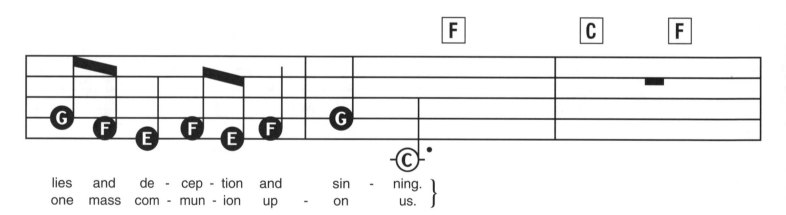

lies and de - cep - tion and   sin - ning.
one mass com - mun - ion up - on   us.

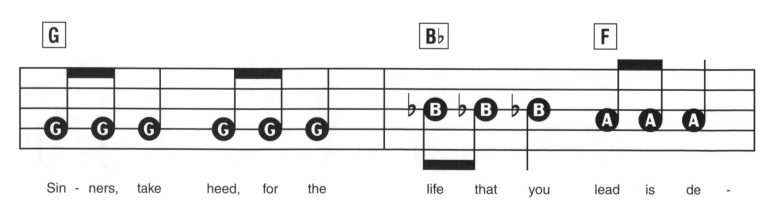

Sin - ners, take heed, for the   life that you lead is de -

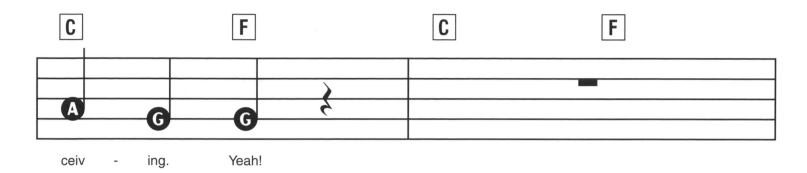

ceiv - ing.   Yeah!

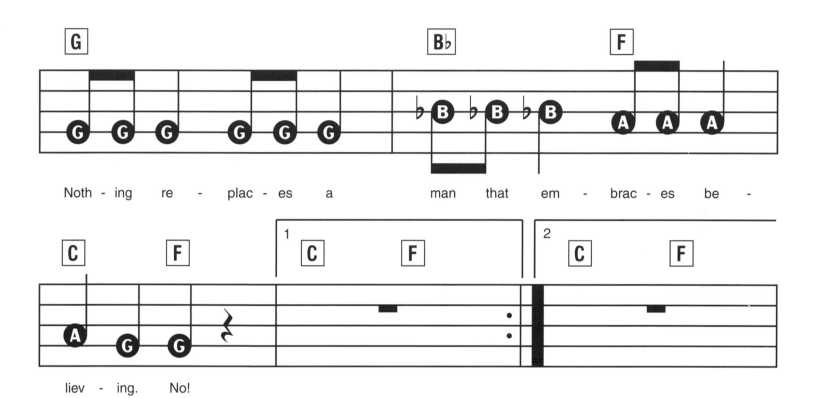

Noth - ing re - plac - es a   man that em - brac - es be -

liev - ing.   No!

I'm bet - tin', I'm   bet - tin' on   Je - sus.

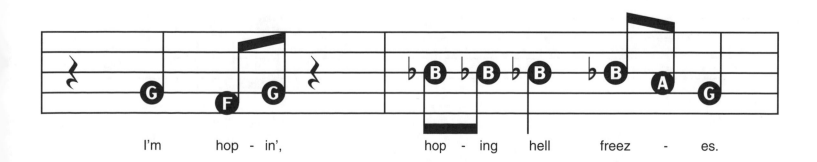

I'm hop - in',   hop - ing hell freez - es.

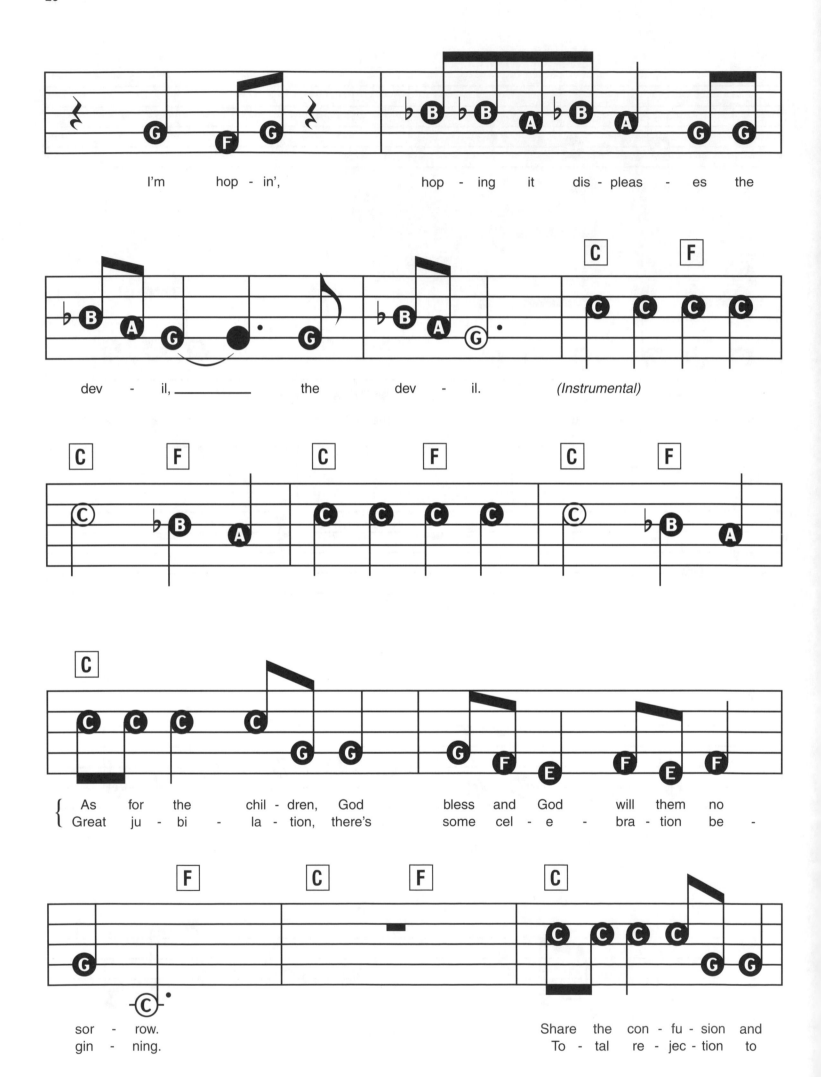

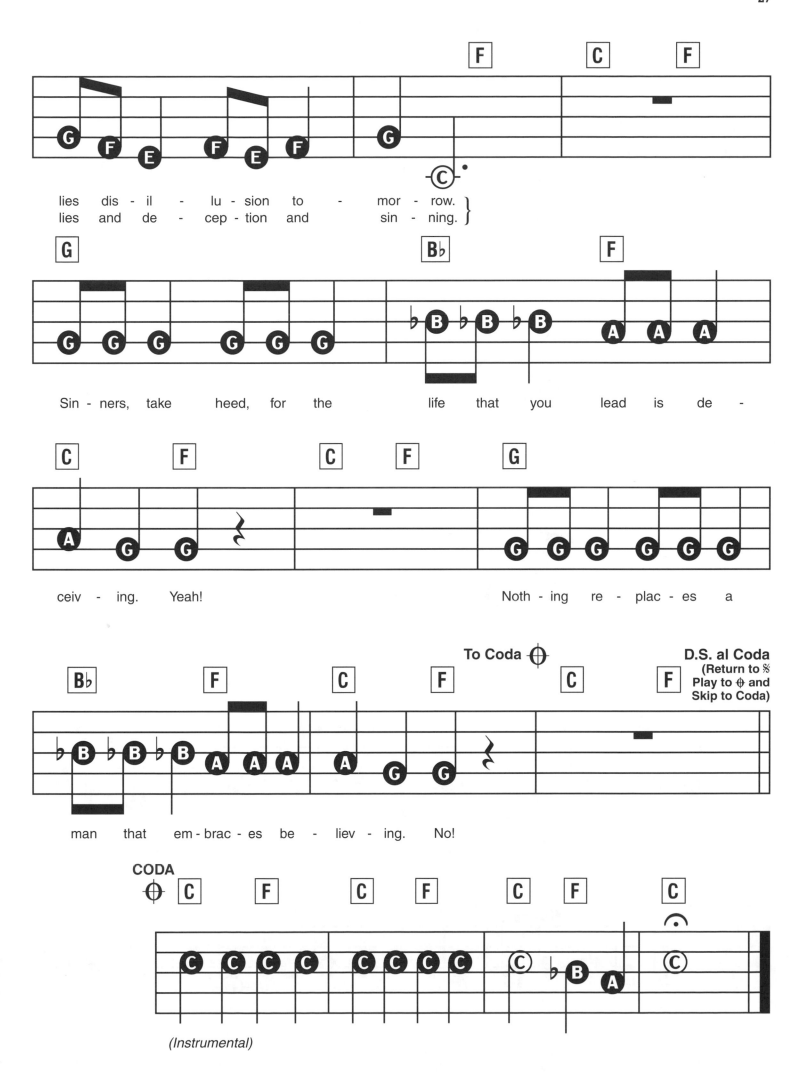

lies dis - il - lu - sion to - mor - row.
lies and de - cep - tion and sin - ning.

Sin - ners, take heed, for the life that you lead is de -

ceiv - ing. Yeah! Noth - ing re - plac - es a

man that em - brac - es be - liev - ing. No!

To Coda

D.S. al Coda
(Return to %
Play to ⊕ and
Skip to Coda)

CODA

(Instrumental)

Lonely Boy

Registration 8
Rhythm: Slow Rock or 12 Beat

Words and Music by
Paul Anka

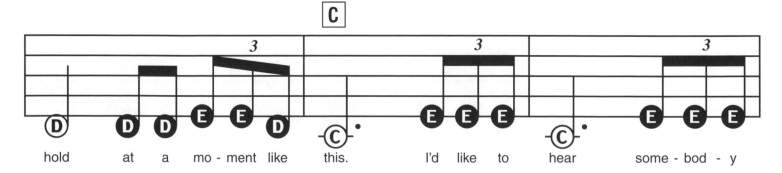

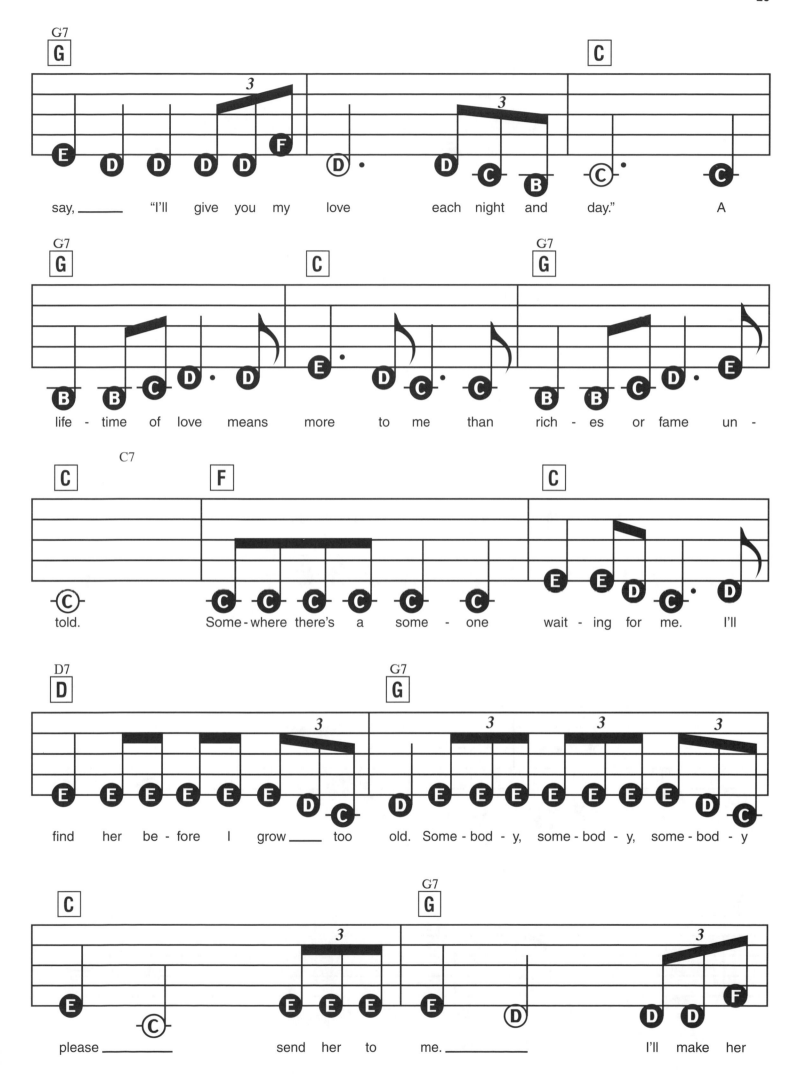

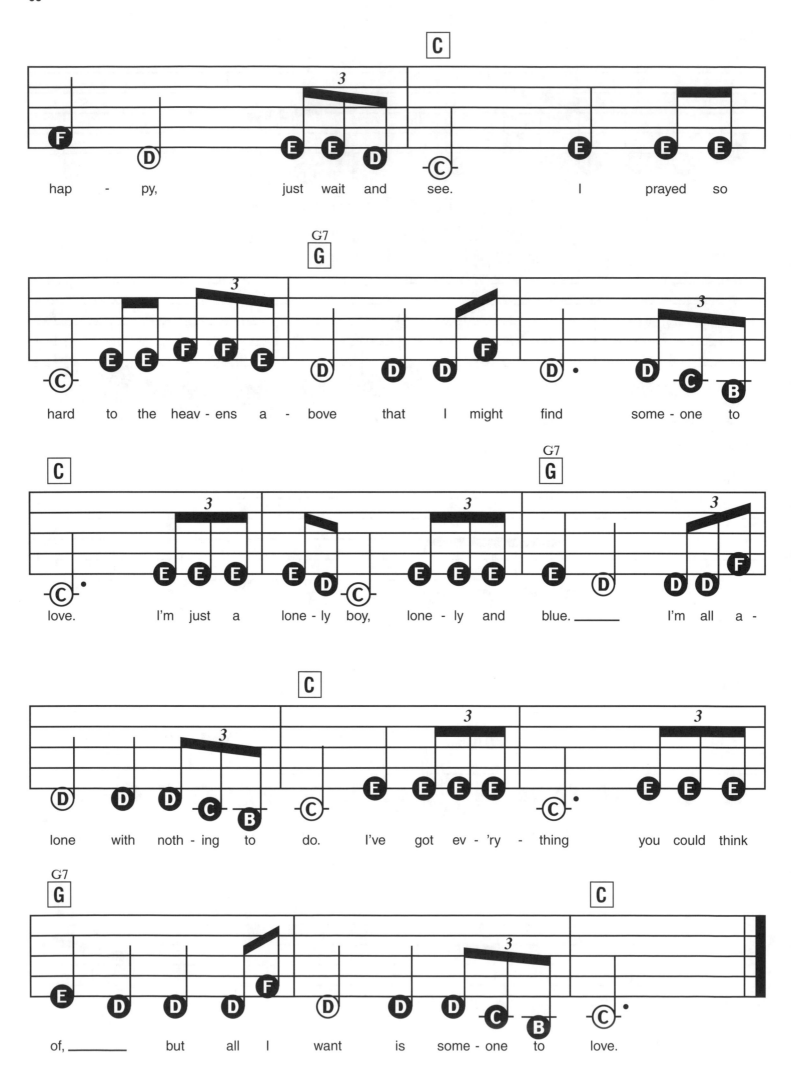

My Way

Registration 5
Rhythm: Ballad or Rock

English Words by Paul Anka
Original French Words by Gilles Thibault
Music by Jacques Revaux and Claude Francois

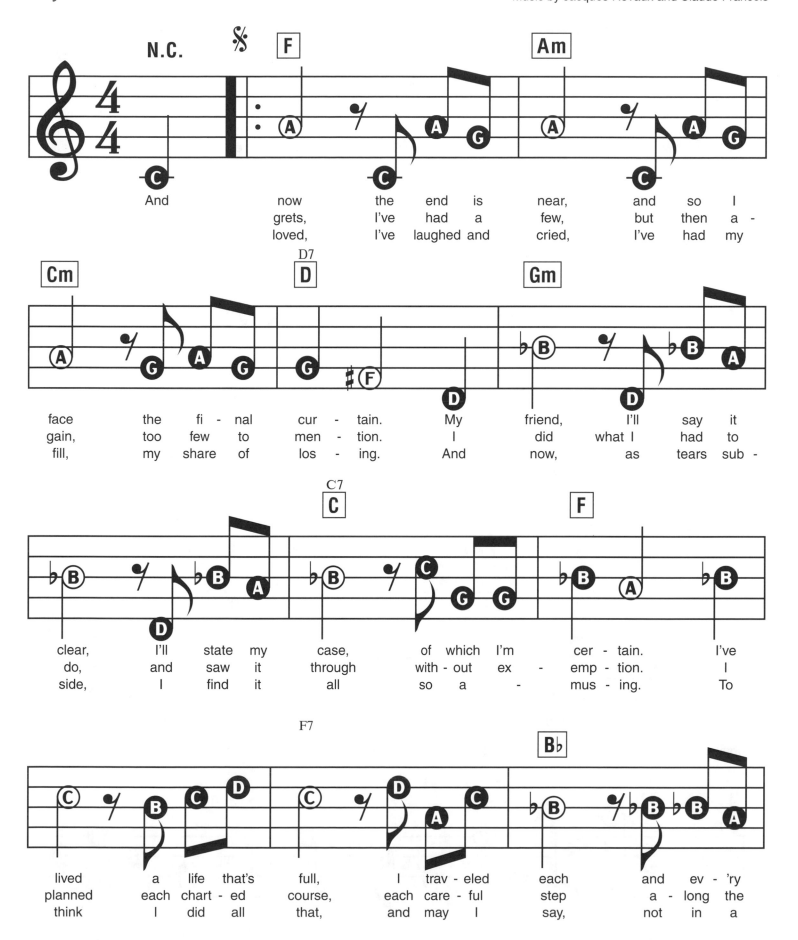

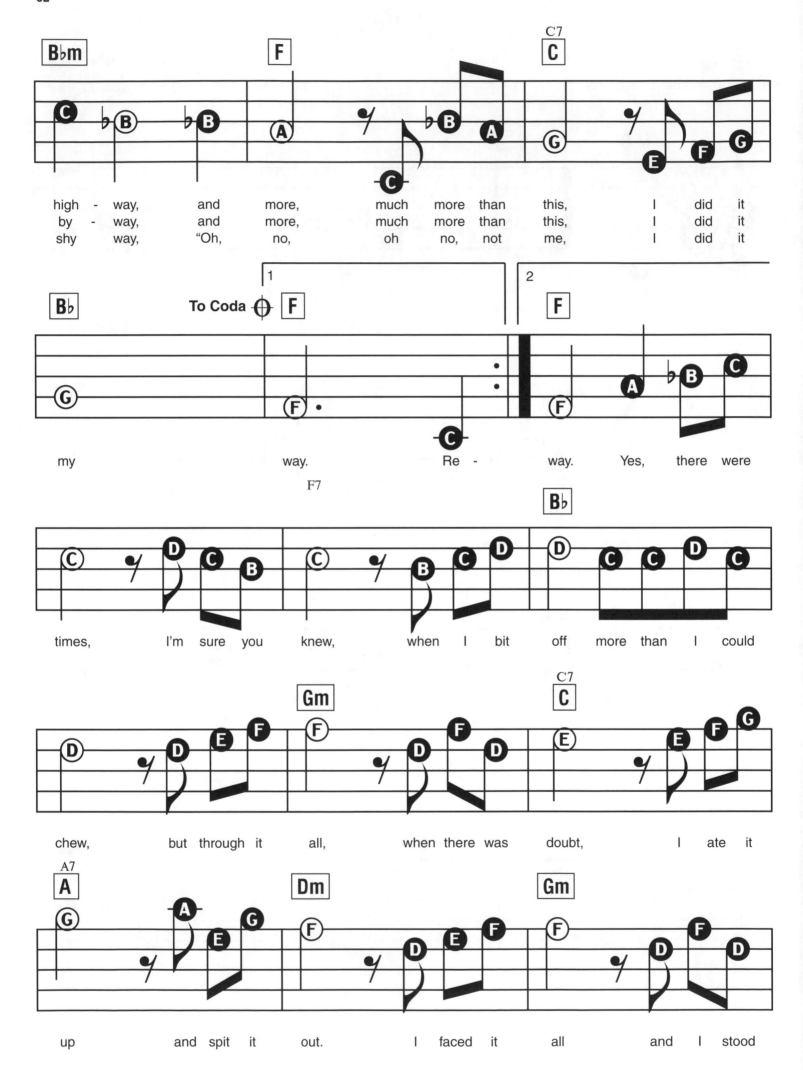

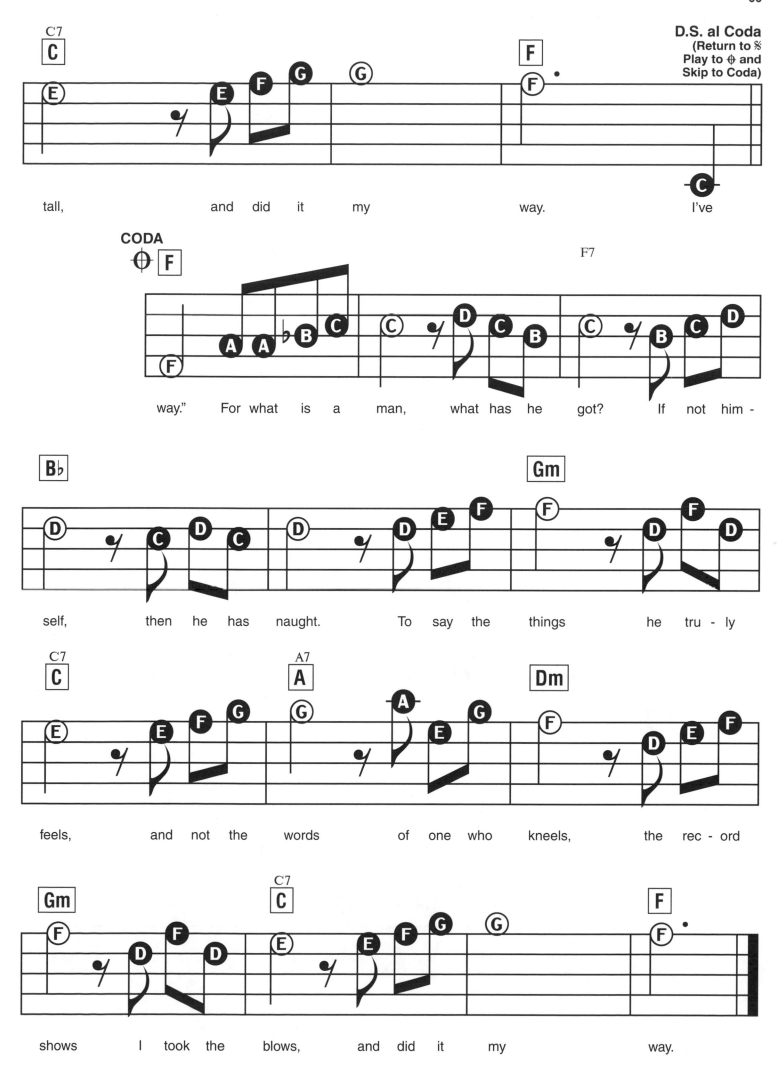

One Man Woman/One Woman Man

Registration 4
Rhythm: 4/4 Ballad or 8 Beat

Words and Music by
Paul Anka

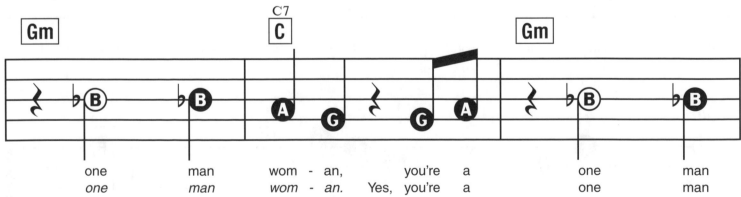

You caught me fool-ing a - round with some-bod-y
*nights you left me a - lone and you dis-ap-

new. You caught me fool-ing a -
peared. The nights your voice on the

round, now I'm los-ing you. _____ 'Cause you're a
phone said, "I'm wait-ing here." _____ *'Cause I'm a*

one man wom - an, you're a one man
one man wom - an. Yes, you're a one man

* All words in italics are sung by a woman.

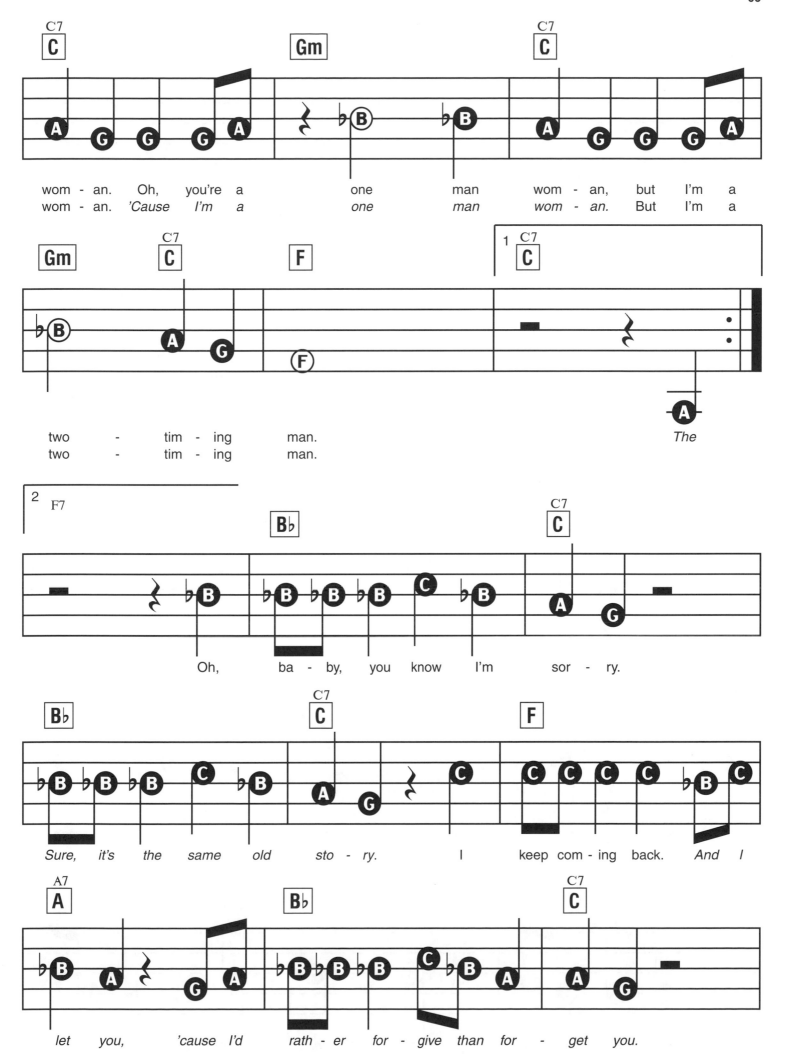

36

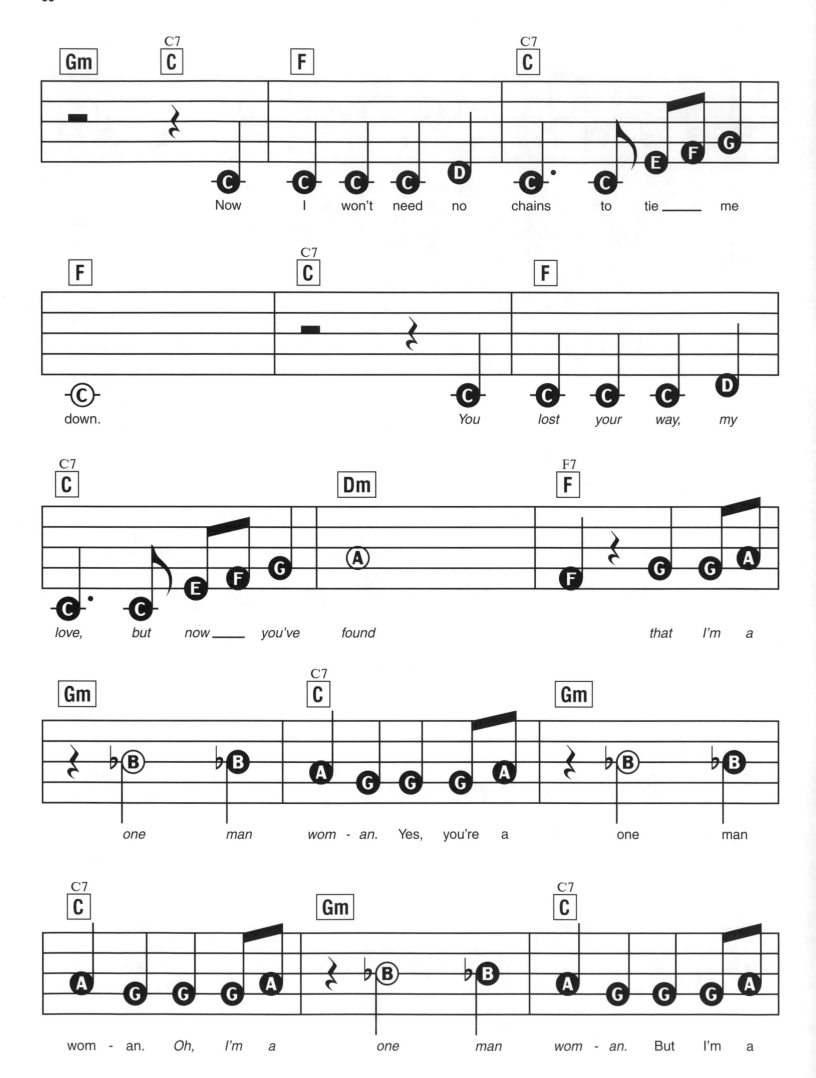

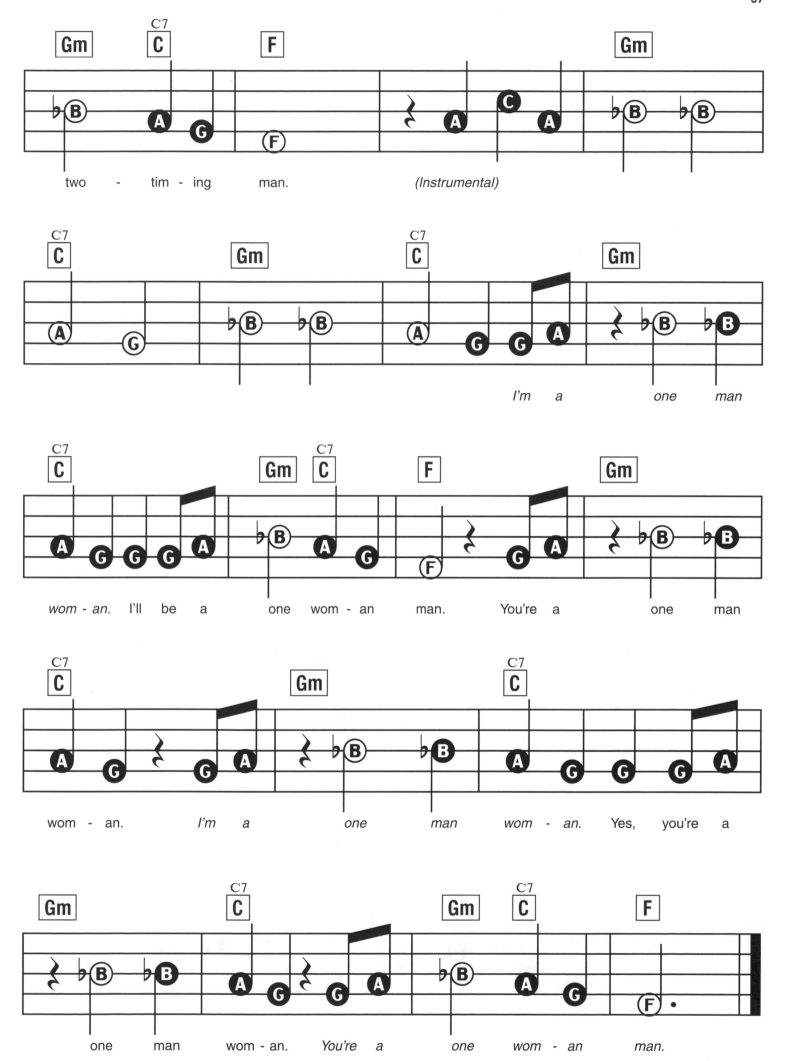

Puppy Love

Registration 8
Rhythm: 8 Beat or Rock

Words and Music by
Paul Anka

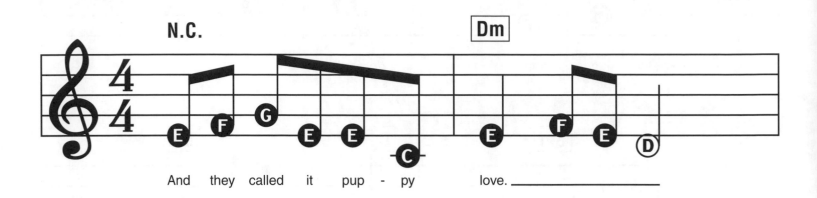

And they called it pup - py love. _____

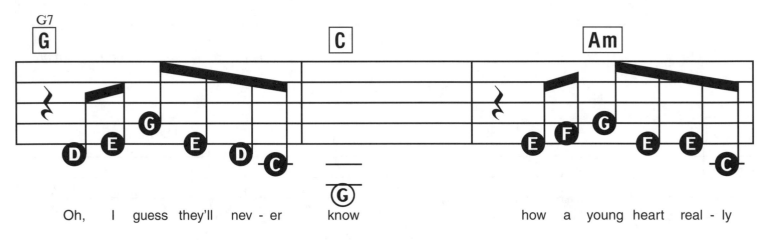

Oh, I guess they'll nev - er know   how a young heart real - ly

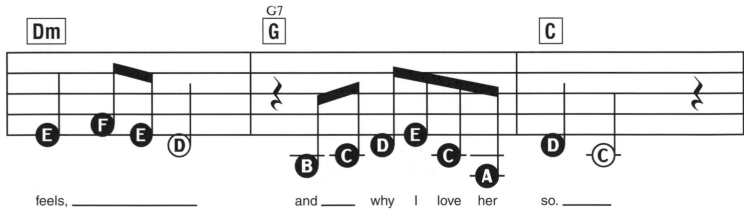

feels, _____ and _____ why I love her so. _____

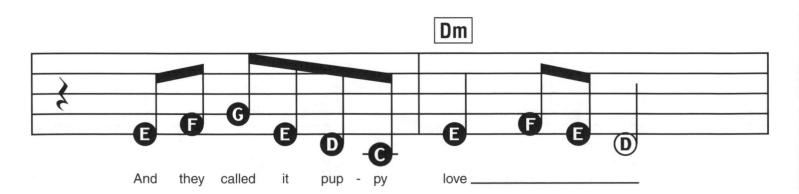

And they called it pup - py love _____

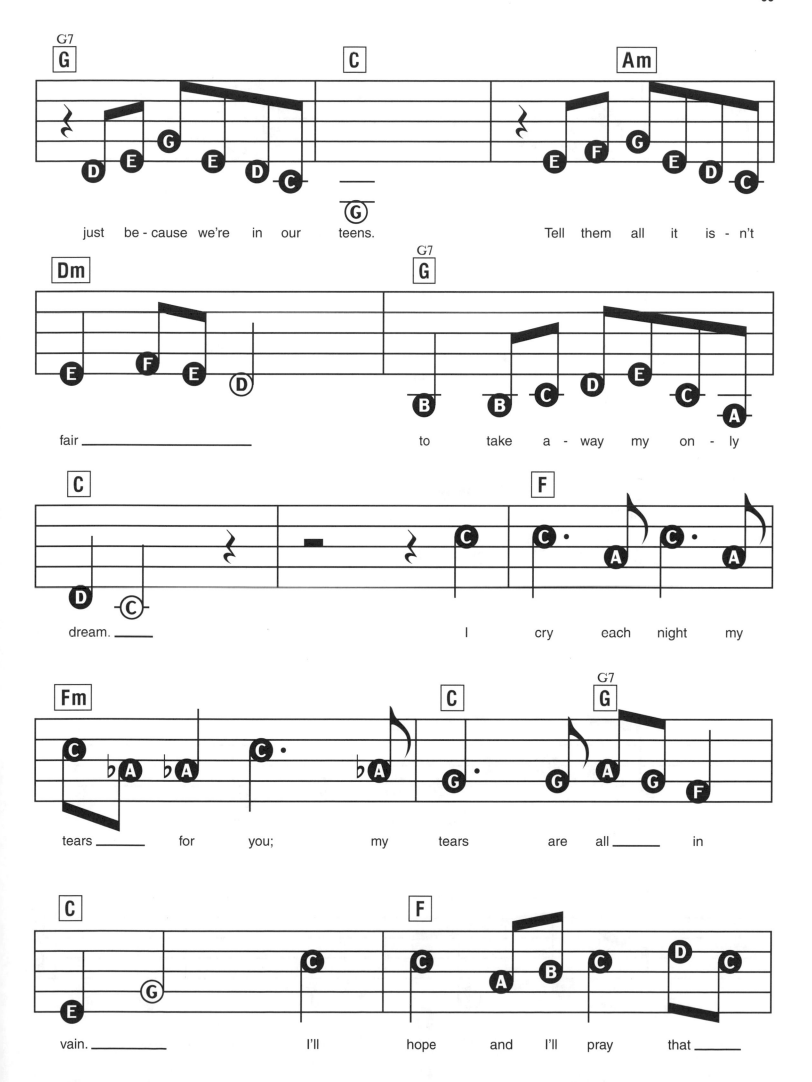

40

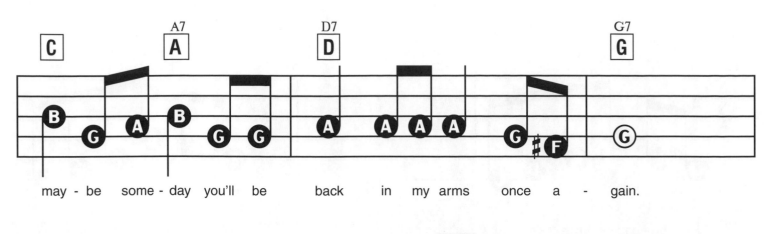

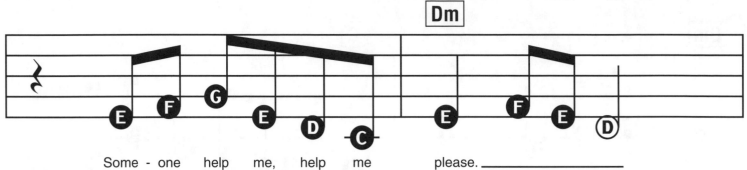

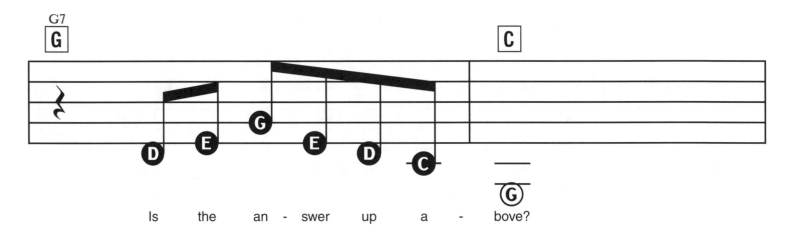

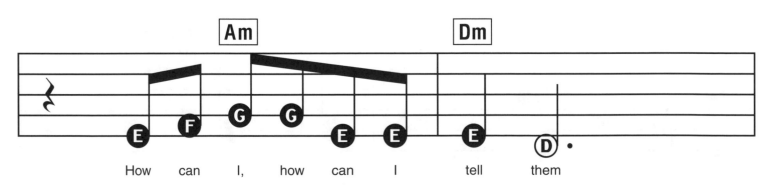

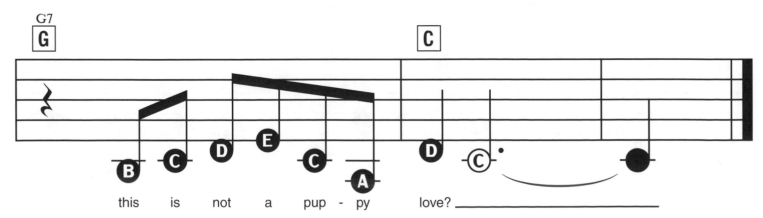

Put Your Head on My Shoulder

Registration 2
Rhythm: Slow Rock or Ballad

Words and Music by
Paul Anka

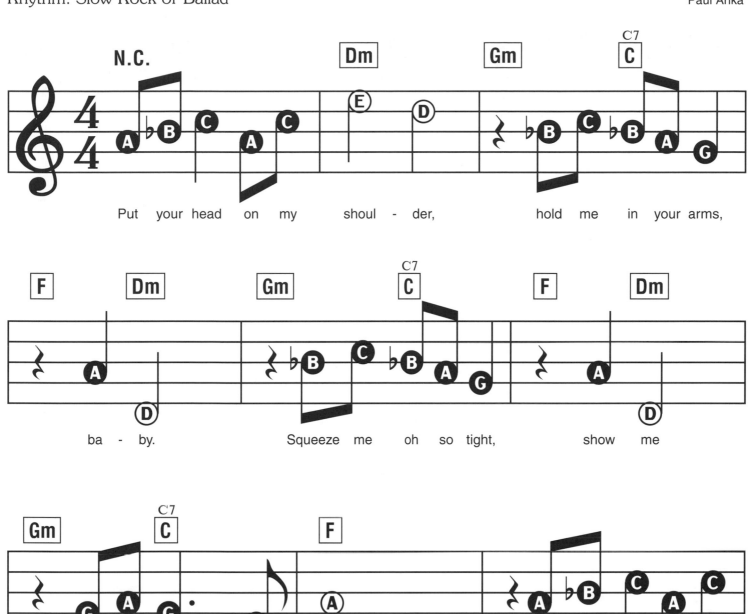

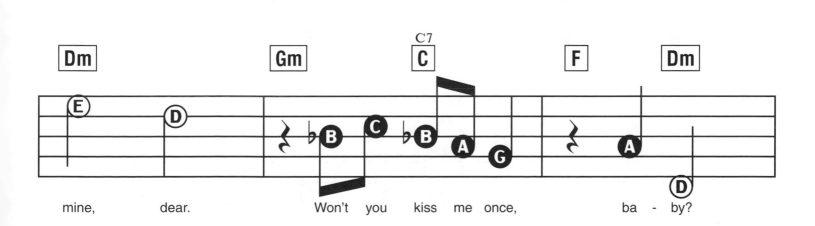

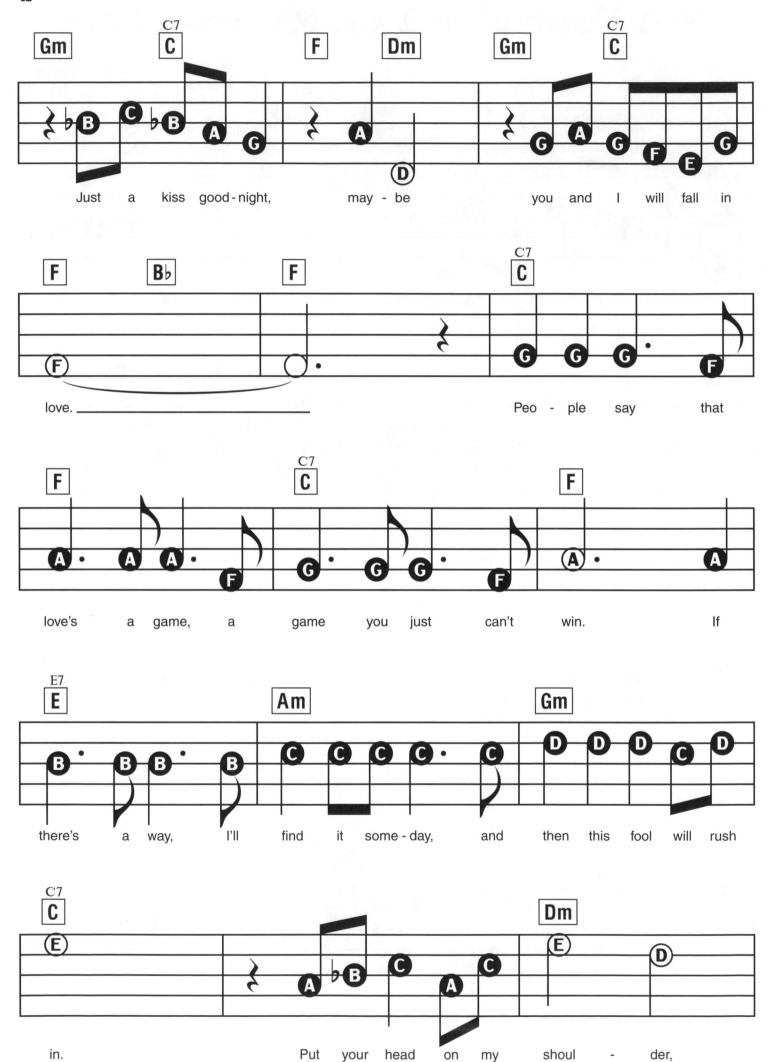

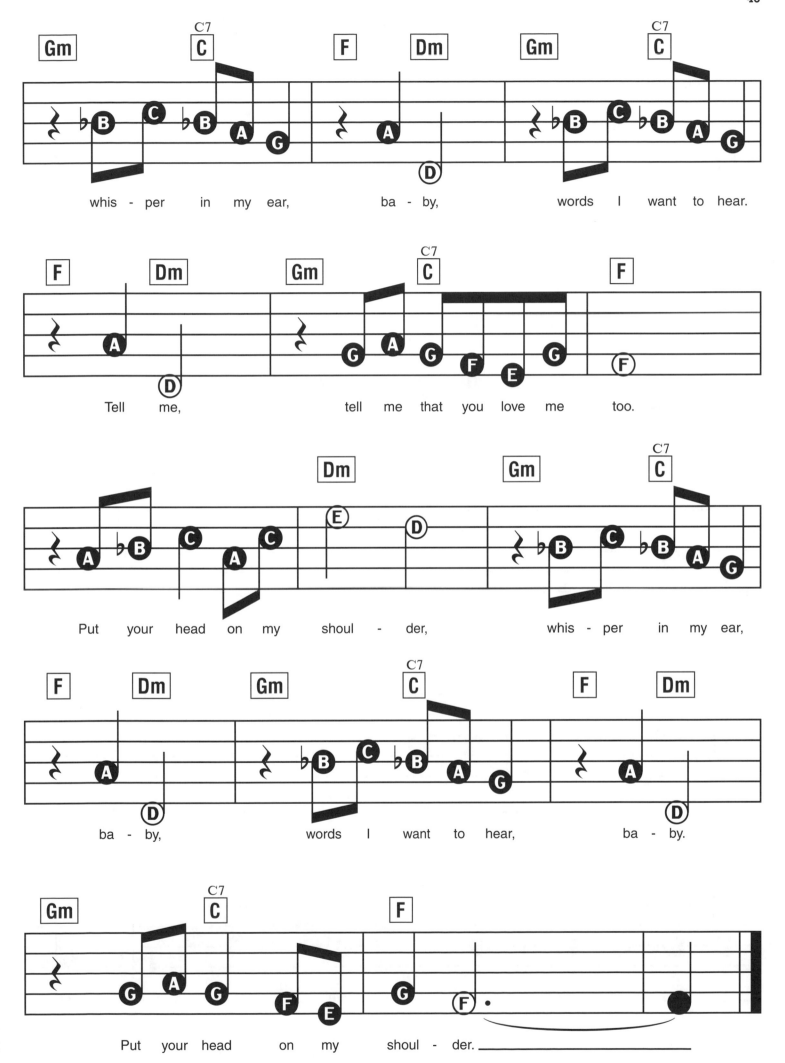

You Are My Destiny

Registration 3
Rhythm: Rock or 8 Beat

Words and Music by
Paul Anka

You are my des - ti - ny, _____ you are what you

are to me. _____ You are my hap - pi - ness, _____

_____ that's what you are. _____ You have my

sweet ca - ress, _____ you share my lone - li - ness. _____

_____ You are my dream come true, _____ that's what you

45

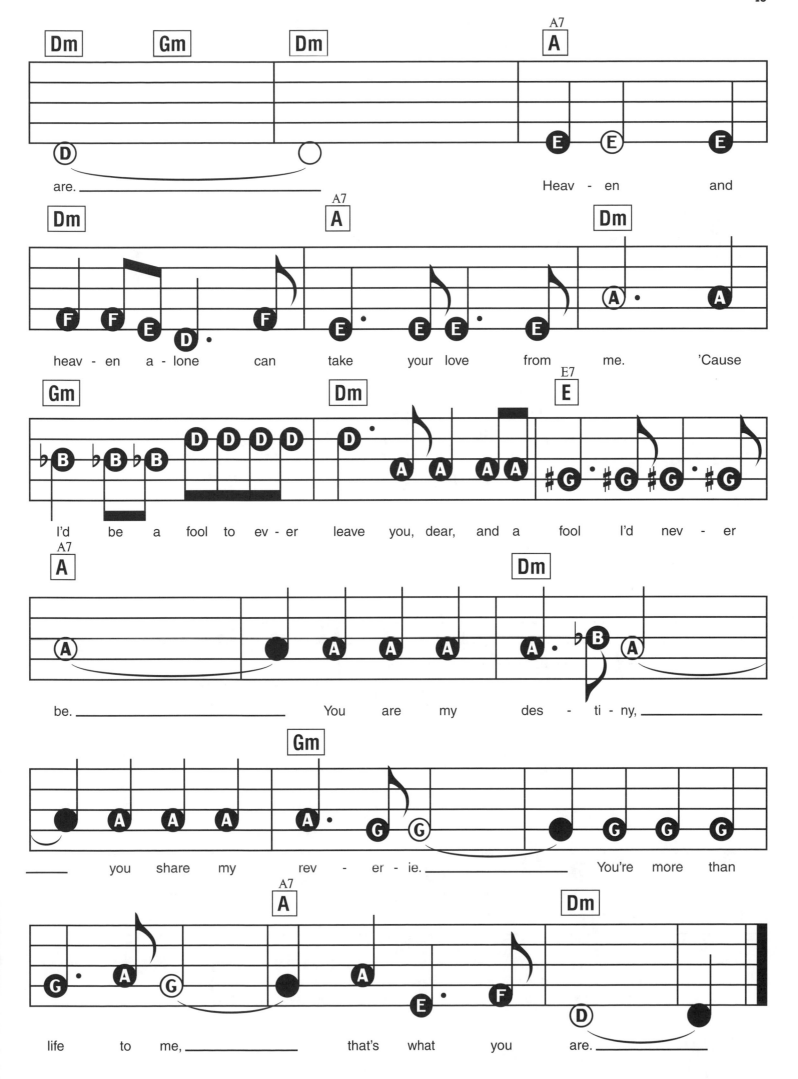

She's a Lady

Registration 7
Rhythm: 8 Beat or Rock

Words and Music by
Paul Anka

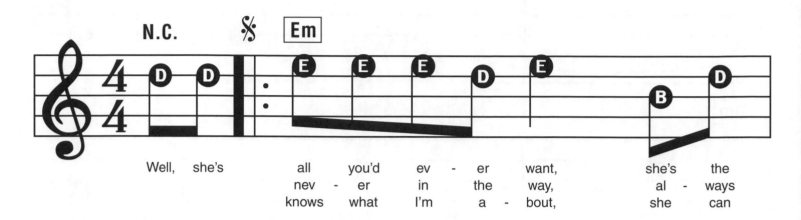

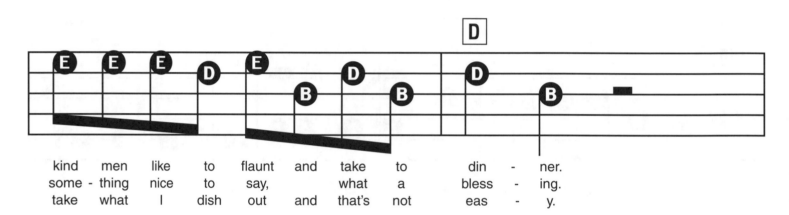

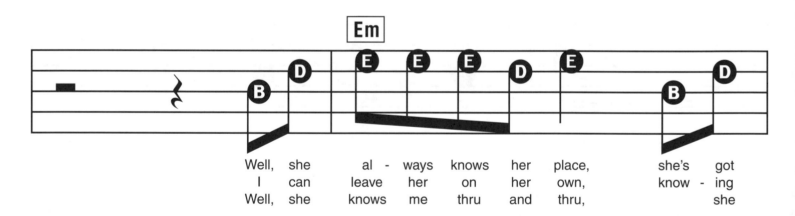

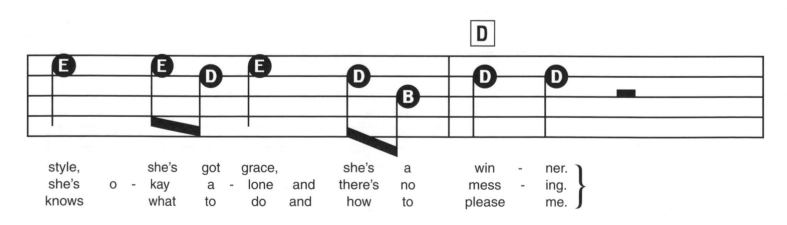

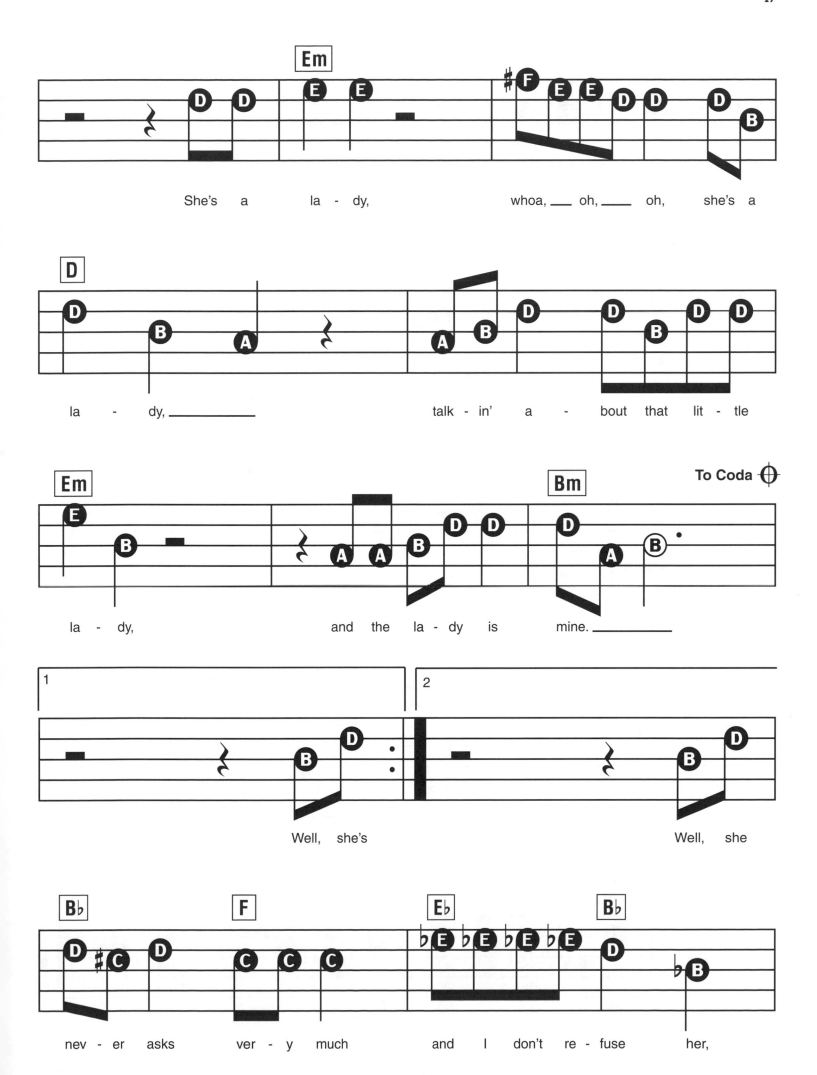

48

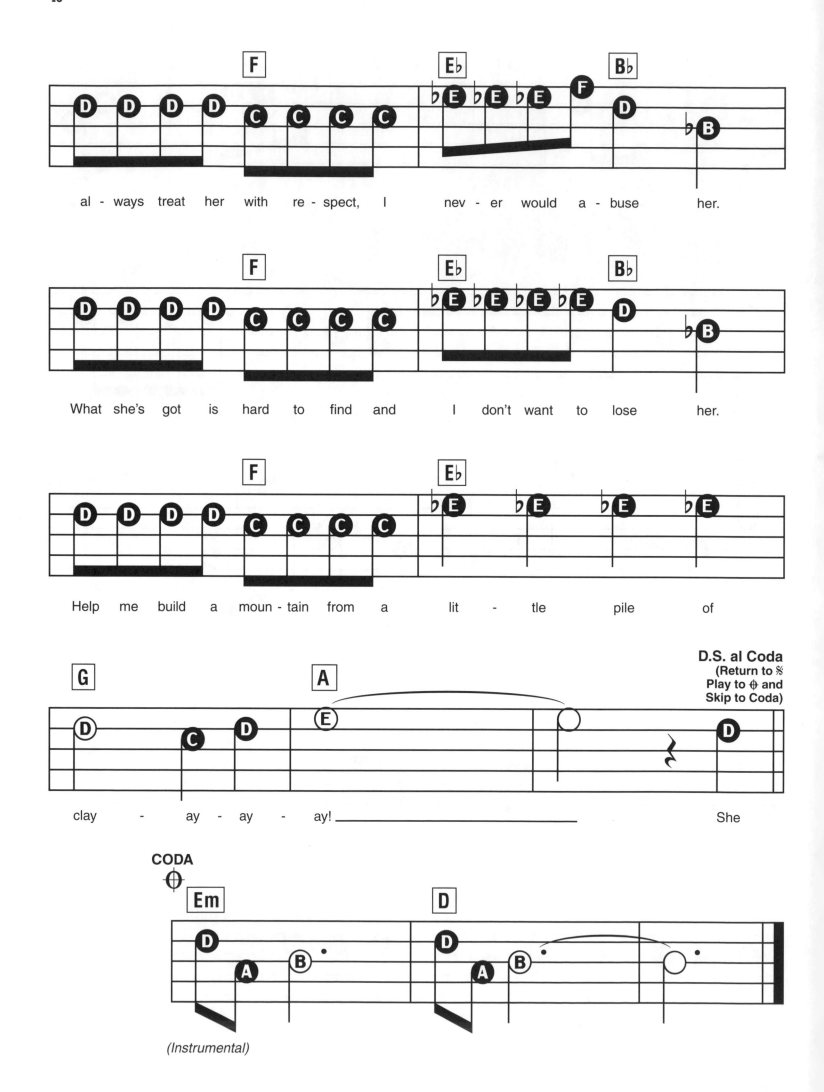

al - ways treat her with re - spect, I nev - er would a - buse her.

What she's got is hard to find and I don't want to lose her.

Help me build a moun - tain from a lit - tle pile of

D.S. al Coda
(Return to 𝄋
Play to ⊕ and
Skip to Coda)

clay - ay - ay - ay! _____ She

CODA

(Instrumental)